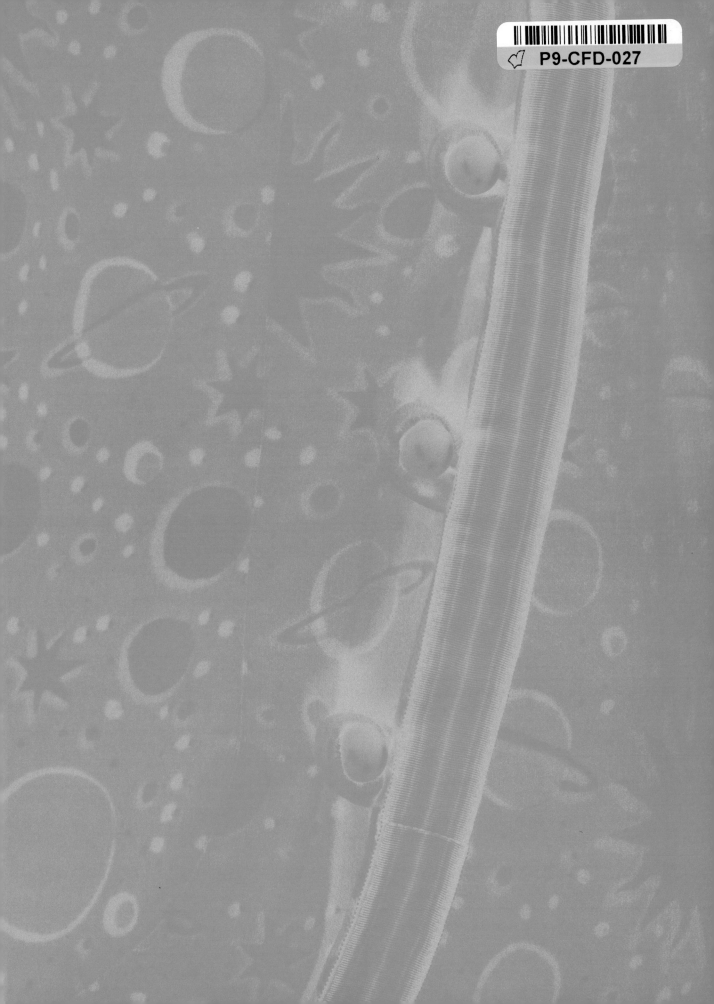

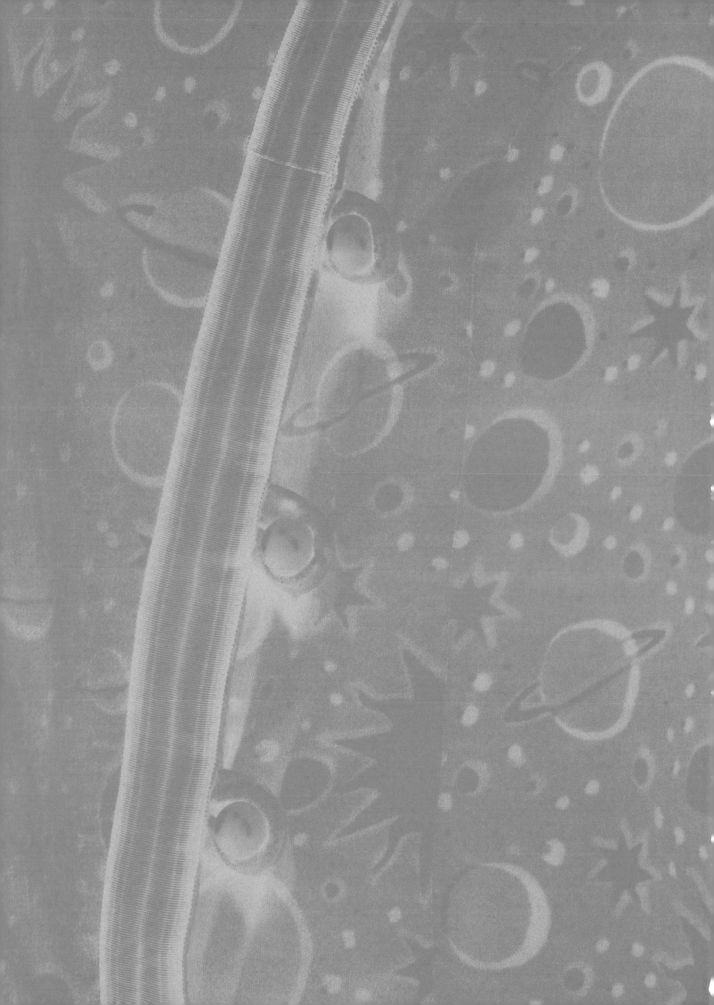

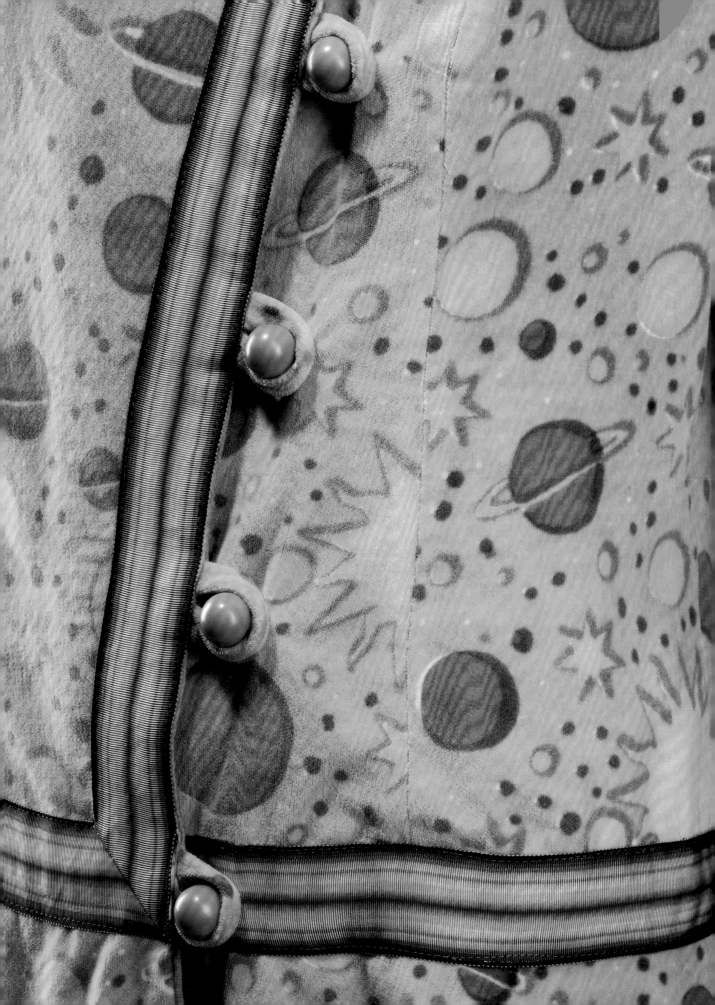

hippie chic

Lauren D. Whitley

MFA Publications | Museum of Fine Arts, Boston

Contents

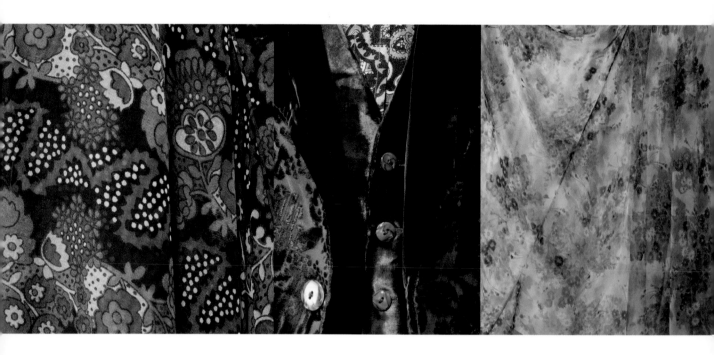

Director's Foreword

The collections of the Museum of Fine Arts, Boston, include more than 45,000 examples of textile and fashion arts, ranging from ancient Egyptian to contemporary and drawing on cultures around the globe. These objects, found at the confluence of art and utility, offer an intriguing way to explore a society's tastes, traditions, and aspirations. *Hippie Chic* revisits a particular cultural moment, the late 1960s and early 1970s in America and Europe, to trace hippies' revolutionary influence on fashion. Innovative young designers and boutique owners, themselves part of the counterculture, translated antiestablishment individualism into artful garments. Their unique fantasy-driven styles in turn trickled up to influence designers of traditional ready-to-wear clothing and even Paris haute couture, resulting in the exuberant "hippie chic" fashions celebrated here.

We are extremely grateful to the many generous donors who have made this book and the exhibition it accompanies possible, including Jean S. and Frederic A. Sharf, the Textile and Costume Society and the Fashion Council of the MFA, Doris May, and Jane Pappalardo. We are also pleased to thank The Coby Foundation, Ltd., for its support of the exhibition, as well as the David and Roberta Logie Fund for Textile and Fashion Arts and the Jean S. and Frederic A. Sharf Exhibition Fund for their additional support. We are ever appreciative of the Ann and John Clarkeson Lecture and Publication Fund for Textiles and Costumes, which supported this book. *Hippie Chic* has been significantly enriched by key loans from private and public institutions. My special thanks to Mr. Peter Brown, Mr. James Raye, and the FIDM Museum at the Fashion Institute of Design & Merchandising in Los Angeles, California, for their contributions.

Malcolm Rogers
Ann and Graham Gund Director
Museum of Fine Arts, Boston

Hippie Chic

From the Street to the Runway

Hippies, swathed in trippy colors, retro fabrics, fur, and fringe, made clothing a canvas for personal expression, forever changing how we relate to what we wear. Their rebellious looks defied the status quo and inspired designers to forge fashions in new ways. Nineteen sixty-five launched a decade of revolution, as social, political, artistic, and cultural conflict transformed life in the United States, Britain, and Europe. The period witnessed the expansion of protests against the Vietnam War and in support of civil rights, as well as the birth of the women's and environmental movements. Youth rebelled against the Establishment and rejected the values and aspirations of previous generations by experimenting with drugs, plunging into the sexual revolution, and rejecting material definitions of success. The young people who would soon become known as hippies adopted long hair and clothing that expressed their wearers' own exuberance, serving as visible symbols of these challenges to authority. The young did not want to live, act, or look like their parents. For the first time, high-end designers weren't dictating all the trends. Instead, many new styles originated on the streets, with the other revolutions, and trickled upward through hip boutiques into the top fashion houses.

Today, thanks to the media legacy of iconic events like San Francisco's "Summer of Love" and Woodstock, we may associate hippies primarily with the United States, but versions of the phenomenon appeared throughout the UK, Europe, and even Australia, forming a "gathering of separate tribes" united by shared values.[1] And while the youth of London, San Francisco, New York, and Amsterdam

Rock star Jim Morrison (standing, center) and his girlfriend Pamela Courson (seated) sold hippie clothing at their offbeat boutique, Themis, which was a popular hangout for the bohemian crowd in Los Angeles (about 1970).

might not have looked exactly the same, they shared a similar ethos, one that emphasized the importance of freedom, personal expression, and fun in fashion.

In America, hippies were predominantly educated, white, middle-class kids, products of the baby boom who rejected what they considered the stultifying boredom of life in cookie-cutter suburban subdivisions. Although some pursued radical and even violent political action, these children of postwar affluence were most broadly aligned against the material aspirations of their parents' generation. Hippies drew on earlier countercultures that produced forerunners such as beatniks, surfers, and folkies. The clarion call had first been sounded by the Beat Generation in the late 1940s and 1950s, and the rejection of conformism and materialism in the work of writers such as Allen Ginsberg, William Burroughs, and Jack Kerouac made them spiritual progenitors.

In their desire to dress in a way that was radically different, young people in the late 1960s widened the chasm between the generations. New York hippie fashion was heavily influenced by the avant-garde art scene, and while it took many of its cues from London's sophisticated urban look, which was distinguished to a large degree by psychedelic references and the eclectic reworking of historical styles, New York also developed its own identity, mixing vintage, designer, and ethnic trends.

At the same time, antiestablishment dropouts and back-to-nature hippies were drawn to the vibrant music scene, mild climate, and relaxed attitudes of California. "The Haight", San Francisco's Haight-Ashbury neighborhood, was a particular magnet for youth interested in exploring the new hippie lifestyle. Some new arrivals established communes for the exploration of alternative lifestyles and a greater connection to nature, celebrating peace and love. Flowers, beads, sandals, American Indian leather and fringe, and colorfully tie-dyed T-shirts typified their laid-back look. By the late 1960s most young people were adopting aspects of the new style. In the eyes of the older generation, anyone with long hair and unconventional clothing was a hippie, but in truth, many who donned the vestments of the movement were thinking less about activism than about accessories.

A seated woman around 1968 mixes a psychedelic flower dress with an earthy leather headband, while a young man, barefoot and dressed in an Indian printed cotton caftan and pants, strides through the grass at the Woodstock Music and Art Fair in Bethel, New York, August 1969.

And while some fervently believed that hippies really would change the world, others were more cynical. The British historian J. H. Plumb critiqued the American phenomenon, declaring that "hippies are largely the waste products of extensive university education systems," and went on to argue that ultimately their radicalism was not as bold as it seemed, for they had "the ultimate safety net of middle-class parents."[2]

In England and Europe, the youth movements that gave rise to hippie culture had a slightly different tenor. The years after World War II had not been so flush there. The new generation came into adulthood still under the shadow of reconstruction and lingering privation. In England especially, austerity measures and rationing laws enacted during the war lasted well into the 1950s. Prosperity finally returned in the 1960s, and once young people had some money in their pockets, a distinctive movement flourished and asserted its own ideas, lifestyle, and, of course, clothing.[3] The elegant, overtly feminine silhouette that had dominated haute couture in the 1950s was replaced by mod (short for "modern") fashion, a minimalist style defined by straight lines and a new creation that particularly suited the burgeoning youth market: the miniskirt.

Prior to this moment, Paris had long been considered the undisputed seat of fashion. Its storied couture houses would create the styles that were adopted and worn by the fashion elite and knocked off by clothing manufacturers. Paris designers Pierre Cardin, André Courrèges, and Paco Rabanne captured the essence of the new mod spirit in fashion with futuristic creations intended for a clientele of rich young women with boyish figures and long slim legs. Yet despite these avant-garde leanings in Paris, a seismic shift took place during the 1960s: London emerged as a new fashion center. With its progressive pop music and trendy boutiques, Swinging London was instrumental in not only initiating but also popularizing the mod look of miniskirts, geometric shapes, and bright colors. Many boutiques sprang up, featuring the work of cutting-edge designers, and their customers were all part of the same subculture and shared the same values and interests. Novel creations by forward thinkers such as Mary Quant, John Bates, and Marion Foale and Sally Tuffin tapped into the tastes and aspirations of an exuberant youth culture. At the same time, the Beatles and other youthful celebrities from England, such as Twiggy, Jean Shrimpton, and Julie Christie, took the world by storm. The British Invasion had begun.

The American fashion scene had long been dominated by a vast ready-to-wear industry of large manufacturers centered on Seventh Avenue in New York City. Their response to the growing youth market that first bubbled up in the 1950s had been to introduce junior lines into existing women's brands. By the 1960s they were only marginally in touch with what was happening on the streets. It took the appearance of unconventional new boutiques, especially in New York, Los Angeles, and San Francisco, to present truly forward-thinking fashions. Shops like the O Boutique and Paraphernalia in New York, which grew out of the local avant-garde music, art, and fashion scene, offered radical designs to customers hungry for them.

Paraphernalia, housed in architect Ulrich Franzen's minimalist glass and steel creation at Sixty-seventh Street and Madison Avenue in New York, showcased the best of the mod styles by British designers. It too fostered home-grown talent like young American designers Betsey Johnson, Joel Schumacher, Deanna Littell, and Michael Mott. Paraphernalia's house model was the actress and socialite Edie Sedgwick, one of Andy Warhol's Superstars and part of his avant-garde Factory scene. Selling ephemeral of-the-moment clothes was vital to the boutique's ethos. Betsey Johnson recalls that she would create a dress out of plastic and aluminum that would likely fall apart after a single wearing, then happily move on to her next design.[4] Johnson eventually left Paraphernalia after it ventured into franchising and founded the boutique Betsey, Bunky, and Nini along with two other Paraphernalia alumni, Barbara Washburn and Anita Latorre. A quirky place where one could find innovative English and European fashions alongside Johnson's own creations, Betsey, Bunky, and Nini encapsulated the unique ethos of ever more anti-establishment fashion emporiums around the globe that rejected peers who became too mainstream. In New York these boutiques flourished in the bohemian neighborhoods of Greenwich Village and St. Mark's Place in the East

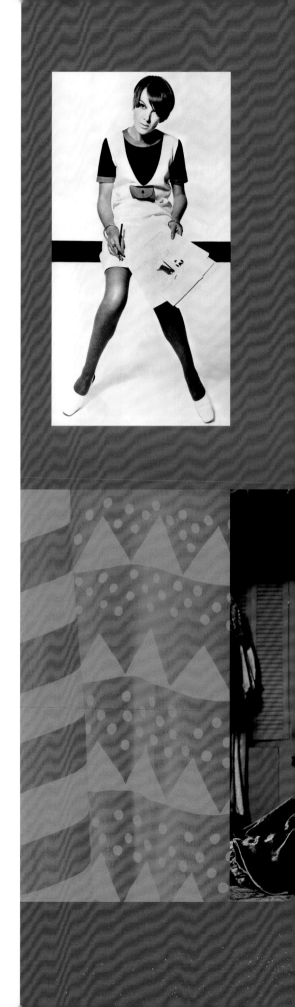

In the mid-1960s, maverick fashion designer Mary Quant created streamlined mod mini dresses like the one seen here on the designer herself (opposite).

Stella Douglas and Colette Mimram opened a nameless boutique in 1968 on East Ninth Street in New York, where they sold trendy English and European fashions. Jimi Hendrix was a frequent customer, as was the musician Johnny Winter, photographed here (standing) wearing an Ossie Clark shirt printed with a Celia Birtwell geometric pattern. Douglas (left) poses in a vintage velvet dress, and Mimram (right) shows off her Ossie Clark fringed ensemble.

Village, even appearing in incarnations so hip they had no name, yet they could also be found all over King's Road, Chelsea, in London, in the Saint-Germain-des-Prés district on the Left Bank in Paris, on Sunset Strip in Los Angeles, and, of course, in Haight-Ashbury in San Francisco.

Instead of copying haute couture designs, the traditional source of new styles, mainstream designers, retailers, and manufacturers began to look to the anti-establishment boutiques for inspiration. Whenever Latorre traveled to Europe on buying trips, "representatives from major department stores [would] tag along after her, asking the stores she [had] visited what she bought and what she declined to buy. And every Saturday, BB&N is filled with designers looking for a quick knock-off."[5]

Traditional Paris haute couture designers were not unaware of the power of this thriving boutique culture, though they were not at the forefront of it either. Young designers in particular took note. In 1966, thirty-year-old Yves Saint Laurent was one of the first of the French haute couture designers to create a ready-to-wear line of his own, called Rive Gauche, in an effort to tap into that vital youth market. Saint Laurent admired the work of English designer Ossie Clark, and may even have taken inspiration from it. According to Jennie Dearden, who worked at the time at the London boutique Quorum, which showcased Clark's designs, somebody from Saint Laurent must have come to the shop, because "in [Saint Laurent's] next collection there was a little Rocker jacket that [Ossie] had done."[6]

An attitude of experimentation, individuality, and personal expression was central to the boutique look. Young people were not merely rejecting the values of their parents but were seeking entirely new experiences — physically, intellectually, and spiritually. Hallucinogens had entered the public consciousness in 1963, when the psychologist Dr. Timothy Leary was dismissed from Harvard University for his controversial advocacy of LSD (dubbed "acid") and psilocybin (known as "magic mushrooms") for attaining enlightenment. To show their support of Leary's stance, Ken Kesey, author of *One Flew Over the Cuckoo's Nest*, and his motley group of LSD-laced acolytes, the Merry Pranksters, drove cross-country in a fluorescent-painted school bus stocked with tape recorders and cameras to document their trip, ending their journey at Leary's Castalia Foundation in Millbrook, New York. Kesey and the Merry Pranksters went on to hold a series of events they called Acid Tests, in which drug use, outrageous "ecstatic" attire, and street performances were encouraged in open defiance of conventional mores. In his "nonfiction novel" *The Electric Kool-Aid Acid Test*, Tom Wolfe immortalized the group's outlandish appearance: "Their faces are painted in Art Nouveau swirls, their Napoleon hats are painted, masks painted, hair dyed weird, embroidered Chinese pajamas, dresses made out of American flags, Flash Gordon diaphanous polyethylene, supermarket Saran Wrap, Indian print coverlets. . . ."[7]

Leary was transformed into a guru of sorts for the burgeoning youth movement. In 1965, when he visited London, LSD was still legal. Leary's British-born associate Michael Hollingshead had preceded him and set up the World Psychedelic Centre in Chelsea, which quickly attracted the cream of the British counterculture — artists, bohemian aristocrats, musicians, and writers, including rock stars Eric Clapton, Donovan, and Paul McCartney, writer Alexander Trocchi, filmmaker Roman Polanski, and art dealer Christopher Gibbs. Soon after, in 1967, thirty thousand hippies converged on the Human Be-In held in Golden Gate Park in San Francisco to hear Leary repeat his famous motto: "Turn on, tune in, drop out."

Fashion, too, became transformative, a means of activating and extending awareness. Fashion journalist Blair Sabol summed up this new attitude in her article for the short-lived avant-garde magazine *Rags*, noting, "It has to do with another plane or dimension entirely, one that has not been seriously considered by the fashion industry in spite of the fact that everywhere this phenomenon called 'Cosmic Consciousness' has been opening up people's minds through drugs, yoga, TM [Transcendental Meditation], and just plain good sex."[8]

In San Francisco, psychedelic clothing may have appeared early on in the form of swirling, colorful tie-dyed T-shirts and painted jeans, but in London, fashions were more sophisticated, owing to the long English tradition of fine tailoring and refined style. Many of the English artists and designers associated with trippy attire, boutiques like

Author Ken Kesey and his Merry Pranksters boarded this psychedelic school bus nicknamed "Further" for their road trip from California to Timothy Leary's headquarters in upstate New York in June 1964.

The Beatles took the world by storm in matching outfits in 1963 (opposite, left). By 1967, Paul, George, Ringo, and John had traded in their staid suits for a more flamboyant style, seen at a press event for the *Sgt. Pepper* album release (opposite, right).

Granny Takes a Trip foremost among them, did not call themselves "hippies" yet, as the term had appeared first in the American press and retained a lingering association with the United States. They did, however, share an attitude toward fashion characterized by increasingly personal, expressive styles and the rejection of minimalist mod geometry. Their psychedelic fashions paved the way for the development of the full-blown hippie look.

The transformation from mod to trippy took place at warp speed. When the Beatles mugged for the camera in 1963, they sported matching mod suits and neatly trimmed hair. By 1967 their starched collars were gone. Instead, the band wore their hair shaggy and posed in an eclectic assortment of colorful prints, velvets, and furs. The Beatles' experimentation with new musical styles was mirrored in their expressive clothing. Their interest in fashion even extended to opening their own clothing shop, called the Apple Boutique.

Young Londoners in general were rejecting mass-produced clothing and pushing the boundaries of mod fashion, experimenting with more outrageous psychedelic styles. Carnaby Street in London hosted a plethora of

British designer Ossie Clark cleverly manipulated a geometric print designed by his wife, Celia Birtwell, to great effect in this retro-inspired dress.

Psychedelic boutique Granny Takes a Trip was notorious for its constantly changing and provocative exteriors. In 1966, its façade was painted with enormous murals of Native American chiefs including Low Dog, an Oglala Sioux chief who fought with Sitting Bull at the Little Bighorn.

boutiques, and came to be known for a new form of colorful, fanciful dress incorporating historical inspirations. Avant-garde fashion also made King's Road in Chelsea, where offbeat boutiques like Granny Takes a Trip appeared, a mecca for artists, bohemian aristocrats, and pop stars. The emerging trippy style had the biggest impact on menswear. Known as the "Peacock Revolution," it was distinguished by a decidedly flamboyant, romantic sensibility—shirts with ruffled cravats, richly colored suits, and Regency or Edwardian-style jackets in showy fabrics like satins and velvets.

Unlike mod fashions, which looked with optimism to the future and the Space Age for inspiration, hippie styles took their cues from the past. A renewed interest in vintage fashions united young people from Australia to San Francisco. For hippies, vintage clothing provided an artful appearance at little cost, and was in harmony with their rejection of materialism and their embrace of the noncommercial. Idiosyncratic items could be juxtaposed with unusual jewelry and accessories to create a playful, unique look that clearly distinguished the young from the old. And while hippies plundered Salvation Army and vintage stores for their colorful "dress-up box" appearance, innovative designers were doing the same thing, combining clothing from different eras to produce the effect of pastiche. Historical fashions from the Renaissance all the way to the nineteenth century were fodder for nostalgic reworking into "granny" dresses, "dandy" suits, and "gypsy" skirts that evoked lush fantasies of bygone eras. Other looks were more tongue in cheek, such as the retro art deco fashions inspired by 1930s Hollywood glamour, or exaggerated 1940s silhouettes worn with campy flair.

The word "ethnic" came to be used as a catchall for the accumulation of textiles, accessories, and clothing from across the globe that were worn alongside vintage fashions. And like the subversive retro looks, these ethnic fashions had more than just aesthetic appeal. An increasing awareness of, and even identification with, the values of indigenous peoples was an important aspect of the counterculture; it was a movement before it became a trend. Back-to-nature hippies, in particular, perceived many "primitive" cultures as more natural than their own, lacking the materialism of corporate-controlled Western society. In adopting their dress, they strove to achieve a better, more meaningful way of life. This aura of authenticity imparted a certain cachet to the wearer, while significantly increasing the rich buffet of fashions available to hippies in their quest for individuality.

The ethnic look was particularly popular on the West Coast, in Los Angeles and San Francisco, and has since become identified with iconic rock stars such as Janis Joplin, Jimi Hendrix, Grace Slick, and the Doors. Fashion critic Blair Sabol discussed the strong connection between music and fashion in her 1970 article "Rock Threads," observing, "Everyone knows that today's fashions are made by people . . . not by magazines or by collection showings . . . but by people who aren't afraid to wear their insides on their outsides."[9] In addition to his signature leather pants, Jim Morrison frequently wore ethnic clothing in the late 1960s. Like the Beatles with the Apple Boutique, he invested in fashion through his boutique, Themis, which offered trendy European clothing and ethnic garb from around the world (see p. 8).

Ethnic clothing opened young people's eyes to

Embracing an eclectic hippie look, Janis Joplin wears gold-embroidered velvet trousers and a cape salvaged from a vintage opera coat. The ensemble was probably made by her friend Linda Gravenites, a designer who created Joplin's stage costumes from 1967 to 1969, many of which mixed ethnic and vintage garments. Joplin sits surrounded by oriental carpets and Indian embroideries.

ancient textile traditions—tie-dye, macramé, knitting, leather tooling—many of which experienced a revival in the late 1960s. Thrifty and creative hippies were taking matters into their own hands, literally; in addition to making their own clothes from scratch, they crafted outfits by modifying secondhand clothes. Many boutique owners and designers themselves started out adapting found garments and fabrics into elaborate outfits. Knitwear designer Kaffe Fassett, who collaborated with the Scottish designer Bill Gibb in the late 1960s and early 1970s, recalled: "Of course it was the hippie time so all the kids were going down to the market, taking an old bedspread, a piece of embroidery from the 1920's and something else from something else and sticking it all together. We were delighted by that; we were doing the same thing ourselves. You'd even buy a dress and turn it into a shirt. It was very free and expressive."[10]

By the end of the 1960s, the ever-changing reinterpretations of so many different themes by hippies, young designers, and boutique owners made it difficult for the large retailers to initiate and control fashion trends. For the first time, the most influential styles were filtering up from the streets to affect mainstream fashion. Critic Marilyn Bender summed up the new regime in 1969, noting: "It was a decade in which the center of fashion gravity shifted from the garment to the accessorized body beautiful, from the Paris haute couture to the boutiques everywhere. Youth was sovereign. Camp dethroned good taste. The rich stole their fads from hippies who rejected materialism."[11] Traditional Seventh Avenue designers including Bill Blass, Norman Norell, Oscar de la Renta, and Geoffrey Beene incorporated elements of street style in their high-end ready-to-wear designs, developing the "rich hippie" look for their well-heeled customers. Paris haute couture, which was equally receptive to influences coming from the youth on the streets, turned out luxurious garments replete with the outward symbols, though not the spirit, of hippiedom, from flowing sleeves to far-out fringe. A long way from its counterculture roots, hippie chic was born.

TRIPPY HIPPIE

The exuberance of psychedelia's anything-goes attitude liberated fashion, opening the door to greater creativity and expression. As counterculture kids experimented more and more with drugs like LSD, commercial art and graphics began to simulate the experience of an acid trip, with its accompanying distortion of perception, its bending, thinning forms, intense colors, and heightened sensuality. Psychedelic light shows played at rock concerts, poster art took on a trippy cast, and fashion was transformed from mere clothing to Cosmic Couture as designers took up an electric palette that incorporated inspirations ranging from acid to art nouveau. Their avant-garde garments featured saturated, often lurid kaleidoscoping colors and contrasting patterns on luxurious textured fabrics that offered lush physical sensations along with their visual shocks.

Groovy Graphics

The flourishing music scene, flamboyant street fashions, and innovative boutiques of Swinging London, the epicenter of all things mod, helped bring the trippy hippie look to life. Many artists moved seamlessly between music, fashion, and graphic arts. The London-based artists' collaborative The Fool not only designed clothing and painted murals but also cut a musical album. At the same time, artist Nigel Waymouth, who co-founded the ultra-hip King's Road boutique Granny Takes a Trip, became increasingly drawn to music and graphic design, eventually abandoning the management of the store to start a design company called Hapshash and the Coloured Coat, which created psychedelic album covers and rock posters, and even produced two albums of its own.

The intense colors, fluid lines, sinuous shapes, and fantastical subjects featured in the posters, album covers,

Model Pattie Boyd, then wife of George Harrison, was an early fan of designs by The Fool. Here Boyd (standing) and two other models strike a pose, wearing the group's colorful fashions in front of a mural also created by the Dutch artist collective (1967).

Victor Moscoso's poster for the Miller Blues Band's concert at the Matrix in 1967 features the vibrating colors of psychedelic commercial art (opposite).

Keiichi Tanaami designed a number of album covers that showcased trippy drawings in saturated hues, including this one for Jefferson Airplane in 1967 (above).

The Fool created the artwork — and the clothing seen in it — for its own musical album, produced in 1968 (right).

magazine illustrations, and animated films by these artists and other luminaries such as Peter Max, Victor Moscoso, Keiichi Tanaami, and Martin Sharp came to typify the look of the late 1960s. Though termed commercial, their images drew heavily on ideas explored in work already accepted as fine art. Pop art's garish colors, collaged elements, and constant appropriation of popular culture both past and present had paved the way for psychedelic graphics, as did

This Alkasura jacket's cartoonlike illustrations, with cat and flower motifs, stippled effects, and candy colors, borrow from the visual language of pop art and psychedelia around 1970. The boutique's co-founder John Lloyd was a famous eccentric who could frequently be seen strolling down King's Road in full monk's habit.

Thea Porter often commissioned artists to design fabrics for her caftans and dresses. Though the creator of this colorful butterfly print from about 1970 remains unknown, the saturated hues and loopy drawing style clearly reveal the influence of psychedelic graphic art.

the experiments with visual perception found in op (short for optical) art.

As the popularity of psychedelic graphics grew, they began to be taken directly from their original two-dimensional form and crafted into fabrics for wearable art. The bright colors and signature loopy lines of Peter Max's posters and advertisements were suddenly appearing on everything from jackets and skirts to umbrellas and ties.

The boutique Alkasura showed a particular affinity for pop art. Founded in 1967 by Paul Reeves and John Lloyd, it was located on King's Road in bohemian Chelsea. The pair's designs drew heavily on contemporary graphic arts, featuring bold prints in saturated colors, and were especially popular with musicians connected with the emerging music genre glam rock, often called glitter rock, embodied in the theatrical dress of pop stars David Bowie and the New York Dolls. Glam rock's pretty boy Marc Bolan of the band T. Rex was notorious for his bright red cherry-print Alkasura jacket. Another Alkasura jacket of printed rayon satin depicts a large cat sitting among flowers.

Though known primarily for her ethnic hippie styles, English designer Thea Porter dipped her toes into psychedelic fashions with a white chiffon dress printed with a vivid graphic pattern of butterflies in fuchsia, orange, and yellow.

Trippy graphics and harsh chromatics reminiscent of LSD trips even appeared on printed dresses by mainstream designer Hanae Mori. Born in Japan, Mori showed a collection in New York for the first time in 1965 and later opened a showroom in Paris. She was known for her elegant, flowing caftans, which often featured her favorite motif, the butterfly. In the late 1960s she created an evening ensemble with a shawl and a one-shoulder romper printed with an enormous face in profile on both its outer sheer chiffon layer and its satin underlayer, which combined to create a moving mirror effect. The colors are intense—yellow, royal blue, hot pink, and orange—and the design resembles contemporary prints in both its color and line.

Cosmic Couture

The cover of the Beatles' 1966 album *Sgt. Pepper's Lonely Hearts Club Band* was one of the earliest popular manifestations of psychedelia. Generally acknowledged as the first concept album, *Sgt. Pepper* featured several novel recording techniques that lent the music its psychedelic sound, from the use of experimental looped tapes of guitars to George Harrison's musical forays with the Indian sitar. Always image-conscious, the Beatles chose to experiment with a concept cover as well. The elaborate photo, created by the pop artist Peter Blake, featured John, Paul, George, and Ringo dressed in colorful satin parodies of military uniforms as their alter ego Lonely Hearts Club Band; they stand in a sea of celebrity simulacra that even incorporated wax effigies of the Fab Four themselves.

Although the Beatles developed the concept of the album cover themselves, it was originally intended to be designed and executed not by Blake but by the band's friends in The Fool—Dutch artists Marijke Koger, Simon Posthuma, and Yosha Leeger, and Canadian Barry Finch. According to Paul McCartney, the Beatles started hanging out with The Fool after buying several pairs of their velvet trousers and jackets. They even commissioned artwork from the collective. As McCartney recalled, "We also liked their graphic work because it was trippy."[1]

It was only logical, then, that after clothing the band and painting John Lennon's piano and George Harrison's

Hanae Mori's evening ensemble from 1968–70 flaunts acid colors.

Members of The Fool were photographed wearing psychedelic clothing of their own design at the Apple Boutique (1968). Much to the horror of Baker Street residents, The Fool had painted the façade of the Apple Boutique in 1967. The mural was soon removed, as no one had secured the proper permits from the local council.

fireplace, The Fool became the main source of psychedelic garments sold at the Apple Boutique, the Beatles' brief experiment with retail fashion. Already a musical juggernaut, the band created the boutique as an emporium for an eclectic collection of paintings, drawings, and decorative objects, described by George and John as "a kind of psychedelic Garden of Eden for lovers of hippie gear."[2] It soon became primarily a clothing store, featuring The Fool's lively printed velvets, satin tunics, trousers, and scarves. Beset by poor management and chronic shoplifting, it survived only eight months, at which point the shop was closed and the stock was given away. Nevertheless, the Apple Boutique continues to symbolize the era's

Husband and wife Yosha Leeger and Barry Finch of The Chariot favored the rainbow palette and celestial motifs seen on this tunic dress from about 1970, produced for their Cosmic Couture line.

changing values: the Beatles, lauded as the greatest band of the twentieth century and credited with revolutionizing popular music, gave fashion their imprimatur as a viable creative outlet.

After the demise of the Apple Boutique, The Fool moved to Los Angeles, where it eventually disbanded. Marijke Koger and Simon Posthuma took to designing clothes for the Summer Sunday fashion line, while Yosha Leeger and Barry Finch developed their own line of Cosmic Couture clothing. In 1970 they opened The Chariot, a boutique on Melrose Avenue in Los Angeles, where they sold handmade clothing and furnishing fabrics to well-known musicians and celebrities, among them Linda Ronstadt and the Pointer Sisters. But the concept of the store went beyond basic business. *Rags* magazine alluded to the greater ambitions of The Chariot, describing it as an "environmental-synergy center," noting "'Cosmic Couture' is the embodiment of spiritual consciousness — using visual symbols in tune with inner harmonies — rainbows, planets, collages of tarot players, swirling flowers, silken brocades. And the colors: all the spectrum in varied patterns, interweavings of texture moving with the body, beautifully tailored, finished with care."[3] A tunic dress designed by Yosha Leeger about 1970 features a fanciful quasi-medieval cut and celestial motifs of stars, moons, and planets silk-screened in vivid colors on cotton velvet, very much in the vein of clothing designed by The Fool a few years earlier for the Apple Boutique. Moving from avant-garde to upscale, Leeger and Finch, her husband,

With its dense floral pattern and intense purple hue, this Granny Takes a Trip velvet suit features the saturated palette and luxurious textures typical of psychedelic fashions (about 1969).

The radiating mushroom on Granny Takes a Trip's label left no doubt as to what kind of trip this granny was on.

eventually shifted to wholesale high-end fashions, selling them under the Cosmic Couture label at luxury department stores Bonwit Teller & Co., Saks Fifth Avenue, and Henri Bendel.

Granny Takes a Trip

Psychedelic fashions with their eye-popping colors were not only a visual feast but a tactile treat as well, showcasing the "interweaving of texture" mentioned in *Rags*. Silk satins and panne velvets, with crushed pile for added luster, were sumptuous to the touch and created a sensual effect. For men the shift was particularly striking, as outfits in these fanciful fabrics contrasted sharply with traditional sober wool suits and marked wearers as both daring and stylish.

Panne velvets were sold at all the influential and innovative boutiques of Swinging London, including Hung on You, Top Gear, Dandie Fashions, and Mr. Freedom. The hippest psychedelic boutique of all was Granny Takes a Trip. Founded in 1966 by three friends, Sheila Cohen, Nigel Waymouth, and John Pearse, it started out selling an eclectic assortment of vintage fashions and became increasingly popular among the young avant-garde. Its ornate interior was atmospherically decorated with patterned Victorian wallpapers and old gramophones and festooned with lace curtains. Waymouth later remarked that at Granny's, he and his partners were "trying to establish a look for people of the underground culture. Our customers were debs, gays, Pop groups and both sexes. It was completely androgynous, we had only one changing room and the clothes were mixed on the rail."[4] Its façade was staged as an ever-changing art installation, painted in turn with a Native American chief (see p. 17), Jean Harlow, and finally its most outrageous display—the front end of a 1947 Dodge bursting through the window. The boutique soon became a trendy haunt, boasting customers who were members of bands like The Who, the Animals, and Pink Floyd. As Granny Takes a Trip escalated in popularity, it added its own clothing line, primarily designed by Pearse, who had trained in London's renowned custom tailoring hub, Savile Row.

Tight velvet garments in extreme colors were staples

A yellow version of William Morris's Bachelor's Button design, first produced by Morris & Co. in 1892, was fashioned into a jacket by Granny Takes a Trip in about 1967. Barry Miles, founder of the Indica Bookshop in London, owned this particular garment (opposite). Noel Redding of the Jimi Hendrix Experience (left) and George Harrison (below) also wore versions of the Morris jacket.

at Granny Takes a Trip, part of the historical dandy look of the period. The fabric could be plain or patterned, as in a three-piece suit made of rich violet velvet, voided in areas to create a dense floral pattern. These velvet suits were not always well made, and the trim cut of the delicate material made them especially prone to splitting at the seams. Or as Pearse himself put it: "You'd become like some tattered troubadour the next day, you know. Some things did fall apart, and everything had to be so tight that seams could burst, especially on velvet. Flimsy cloth. . . ."[5]

The most famous jacket produced by Granny Takes a Trip was a floral number that could be seen all over the streets of London on rock musicians and artists in the late 1960s. Rock guitarist Noel Redding, George Harrison, Nigel Waymouth, and even the fashion designer Ossie Clark were photographed sporting different versions of it. Designed by Pearse and tailored at the Foster City Road Tailors, it was made from furnishing fabrics originally designed by William Morris in the late nineteenth century. For fifteen guineas, some 250 dollars in today's currency, buyers could choose from several different patterns and colors.[6]

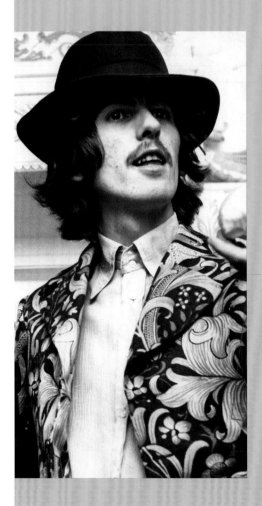

Acid and Art Nouveau

The William Morris jacket signaled the revival of interest in late-nineteenth-century art that was percolating in the late 1960s. Pearse recalled: "We were dealing in vintage clothes. What appealed to us was Aubrey Beardsley and the Victorians, *Against Nature* by Huysmans. So we were all doomed Romantics at that time, NOT new Romantics, doomed Romantics. So that was the influence — Art Nouveau."[7] This fixation on the art of the late nineteenth century, and on art nouveau in particular, reflected a rejection by youth of the clean lines of modernism. With their sinuous twisting shapes, decorative ornament, and erotic subtext, art nouveau graphics were an appealing mirror image of the contemporary drug experience.

The late-nineteenth-century influence on fashion was apparent in the widespread adoption of floral patterns, which took the form of William Morris motifs from the Arts and Crafts era, as with the Granny Takes a Trip jacket, and the ubiquitous paisley, formerly associated with Victorian shawls. Ken Scott, an American designer working in Italy, was renowned for his deftness at rendering flowers on fabric. In the late 1960s, he produced a number of clothing and furnishing textiles incorporating the new palette and graphic style of psychedelic art. A length of Scott's cotton velvet called Coquelicot was printed with electric red and orange poppies on a hot pink ground. While the oversize flowers are reminiscent of late-nineteenth-century styles, the acid colors and the potent connotation of the flowers themselves offer a playful allusion to the drug experience. Scott's dense floral design would have been understood as a contemporary take on Stile Liberty, the term used in Italy for art nouveau. The Italian movement was named for Liberty of London, the British company that originally produced the prints, and which itself experienced a revival in the late 1960s after its design director, Bernard Nevill, reworked traditional nineteenth-century Liberty floral prints to reflect the new psychedelic hues and patterns.

Large poppies in trippy colors populate Ken Scott's Coquelicot printed velvet (late 1960s), while the shiny satin and jarring blue and orange print make Yves Saint Laurent's pantsuit for winter 1971 a sensory feast.

The pattern on this man's shirt from about 1970 was adapted from two art nouveau posters, including an advertisement designed in 1895 by William Bradley (left).

The trippy trend even crossed the channel to Paris, where Yves Saint Laurent experimented with bold graphic prints on a satin suit created for his Rive Gauche line in 1971. The print's stylized trees and stippled shading effects likewise evoke art nouveau drawings, while the lurid contrast of royal blue and orange generates an eye-popping energy.

Designers could be quite literal in their adaptations of art nouveau, inspired by major exhibitions in London of the work of Aubrey Beardsley, Henri de Toulouse-Lautrec, and Alphonse Mucha. The patterns on a man's shirt from the late 1960s were taken directly from two separate late-nineteenth-century prints. The stylized figure of the woman on a bicycle first appeared in a lithograph created by an American artist, William Bradley, for the Victor Bicycles Company in 1895, while the text that appears above it, rendered in distinctive turn-of-the-century type, comes from one of the posters created by the prolific Swiss artist Théophile Alexandre Steinlen in the 1890s.

With its signature sinuous forms, art nouveau typography resonated with artists who wanted to capture the trippy drug experience in print. Before long the psychedelic style would sour, a victim of overexposure and too many bad trips from which superstars of the youth culture never returned. In the meantime, by looking backward, young designers found new ways of pushing fashion forward. The burgeoning interest in historical decoration embraced period fashions as well, which would be taken up with enthusiasm in the late 1960s.

FANTASY HIPPIE

dwardian dandies, Renaissance troubadours, Victorian maidens, and other figures from the past suddenly began to appear on the streets of London, New York, and San Francisco in the late 1960s. Their fantastical outfits originated as a countercultural statement, a mildly subversive thumbing of the nose at contemporary society's conservative dress code. Hippies were drawn to the cheap prices of vintage fashions, but also to their potential for playfulness and the shock value of appearing in clothing radically different from that worn by "straight" society. As an article in *Rags* magazine noted, "old clothes have a marvelous way of horrifying the people you want to horrify, while delighting the people you want to delight."[1] Historical fantasy dress could also transform the wearer into someone new by channeling an idealized vision of the past. Such clothing became a liberating way of making daydreams a reality on the streets as well as in high society.

The Dandy

Men's fashions of the late 1960s quickly adopted popular elements of fantasy. London's avant-garde boutiques led the way with flamboyant shirts and suits, sparking what was dubbed the Peacock Revolution. Regency looks evoked England's most famous dandy, Beau Brummell, whose meticulously elegant attire influenced men's fashions in the early nineteenth century. In turn, twentieth-century dandies wore ruffled shirts and lace cuffs that verged on the feminine, along with cravats, striped jackets, and colorful velvet suits. Elaborate in design and tailored snug to the figure, they were a bold departure from the sedate gray flannel suits of the 1950s and early 1960s.

Bespoke, or custom-made, dandy suits with an outrageous edge were the specialty of Michael Fish, a

Scottish designer Bill Gibb's Woodland print dress was one of his most fantastical designs, featuring an all-over pattern of trees crafted into a quasi-medieval gown with full sleeves (*Brides*, September 1972).

Savile Row–trained tailor who in 1966 opened a boutique called Mr. Fish on Clifford Street in Piccadilly. The eclectic shop was full of "see-through voiles, brocades, and spangles, and mini-skirts for men, blinding silks, flower-printed hats."[2] Photographer and man about town Patrick Lichfield (Thomas Patrick John Anson, fifth Earl of Lichfield), a frequent customer, wore his romantic shirts with great aplomb. Even Mick Jagger adopted the look, causing a sensation in the press when he wore a Mr. Fish ruffled smock tunic during the Stones' Hyde Park concert in 1969 dedicated to Brian Jones.

The London boutique Granny Takes a Trip created its own versions of the dandy suit with bold patterns and flashy fabrics more in spirit with England's other notorious dandy, Oscar Wilde. One suit was striped in orange and purple silk satins, accompanied by wide lapels, contrasting black velvet on pockets and collar, and matching purple trousers. Granny Takes a Trip also produced suits made of contrasting colored velvet panels and cut long, in the Edwardian style. Such panel jackets were particularly popular among pop stars in the early 1970s; Rod Stewart allegedly wore one for his appearance on the British television program *Top of the Pops* in 1971.

The Granny Dress and the American Frontier

Young women likewise looked to an earlier era, sporting turn-of-the-century gowns salvaged from thrift stores and antique shops. In reworking elements of period dress — high collars, puffed sleeves, and flounced skirts — designers were responding directly to the power of street style. Romantic fantasy dresses were the specialty of English designer Gina Fratini. A graduate of the Royal College of Art, she opened her business in 1964 and joined the thriving boutique scene during the heyday of Swinging London. Her transition to the new, longer styles of the late 1960s can be seen in her reworked baby doll dress, which retains the low neckline and high waist of earlier mod fashions grafted to a floor-sweeping "granny"-length skirt. Another English designer, Laura Ashley, built a successful business based entirely on the Edwardian-inspired granny style, evoking the charm of country life with flounced and

Patrick Lichfield, a successful photographer described in *Vogue* as a "smashing dresser, with his own particular brand of elegance" (November 1967), appears in an ornately embroidered jacket, a Byronesque shirt by Mr. Fish, and a silver-buckled Annacat belt.

After Mick Jagger (opposite, top) wore this daring Mr. Fish tunic in front of a crowd of 250,000 fans, *Vogue* sardonically reported it was "now being knocked off all over London . . . for girls" (September 1969).

Granny Takes a Trip designed this striped suit and panel jacket, both in the Edwardian dandy style (about 1969–70).

ruffled gowns in simple white cotton and old-fashioned floral prints.

American designers also plumbed this nostalgia for simpler times, often drawing on the country's frontier past for inspiration. The idealized interpretations of nineteenth-century American clothing realized in the "prairie" dress, their variation on the granny gown, were in step with the growing back-to-nature movement of the late 1960s and early 1970s. In 1969 the *New York Times* declared that the trendy young urban woman was enthusiastically embracing the new old look: "Her false eyelashes have been tossed on the pile of fashion debris that includes space-age helmets, plastic tutus, and deer hunter's buckskin. Her hair is pulled up on top of her head, as in portraits of grandmother. And when she walks, her petticoat skirts rustle, her sleeves flounce and she might even show a bit of lacy pantelet."[3]

In addition to reviving older silhouettes, designers reworked nineteenth-century fabrics. In September 1970 *Women's Wear Daily* announced to its readers, "Chintz is back in fashion," while *American Fabrics* hailed the return of "romantic challis."[4] Small-scale floral calicos and chintzes, as well as ginghams, laces, and wool plaids, were the materials of choice in prairie dresses. The American

English designer Gina Fratini excelled at creating granny dresses, as seen in this late 1960s example (above and right), which features dotted swiss cotton embroidered with tiny floral sprays and delicate lace trim around the low neckline.

Turn-of-the-century charm, complete with flounces and cotton eyelet, graced the pages of *Vogue*'s November 1968 issue in an editorial called "The Romantic Contenders — Freshly Edwardian" (opposite).

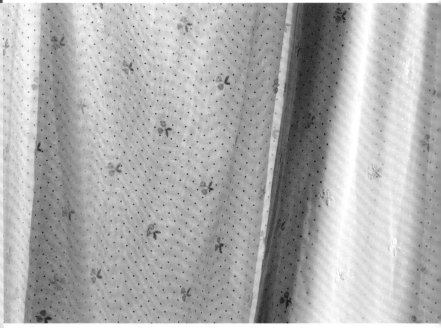

Opposite, a red and white gingham
prairie dress from Adolfo (about 1970)

In February 1970 *Vogue* reported from
Los Angeles, "Girls out here love the
sidewalk-dusting day dress too" (right).

Betsey Johnson's 1968 Tara dress was
celebrated for its "layers and layers of
ante-bellum romance" (below).

designer Adolfo created a two-piece dress out of red-and-
white-checked cotton gingham, a humble fabric that was
likely intended to conjure up images of America's frontier.
The homestead is further implied in the silhouette of the
dress. The high standing collar, leg-o'-mutton sleeves,
peplum, and floor-sweeping skirt trimmed with a deep
ruffled flounce evoke styles of the 1890s.

Traveling far from the futuristic silver and plastic
miniskirts she created in the mid-1960s, even Betsey Johnson explored the nostalgic look a few years later while still
designing for the avant-garde New York boutique Paraphernalia. Her Tara dress from 1968 takes fanciful inspiration from the full-skirted mid-nineteenth-century fashions
romanticized in the popular American novel *Gone with the
Wind,* and from the elaborate costumes in the movie based
on it. A one-piece dress of brown cotton printed with floral
sprigs, it features a deep, round neckline, long sleeves with
flaring cuffs, and a full skirt trimmed with three layers of
gathered flounces.

The Gypsy

Whereas Edwardian white cotton dresses conjured fairy-tale innocence and "everything to make a girl feel fragile and adored,"[5] gypsy dresses tapped into a more daring and exotic fantasy. By combining colorful folk costumes with romantic flourishes such as layered flounced skirts and clashing patterned fabrics, they offered rich opportunities for playing dress-up. In the early 1970s, Thea Porter created her own version of the gypsy dress in printed chiffon. The short, notched bodice is trimmed with gold braid in a style reminiscent of eastern European or Balkan folk costumes, while the handkerchief hemline on the skirt of yellow and purple printed chiffon lends an additional dramatic touch.

American designer Giorgio di Sant'Angelo's 1969 collection focused exclusively on the gypsy look: poufy silk pants, boleros, flounced blouses, and brightly crafted belts

A gypsy dress designed by Thea Porter (around 1970)

Model Jean Shrimpton appeared in *Vogue* (March 1969) wearing one of the dresses from Giorgio di Sant'Angelo's first collection, which featured multiple skirts over embroidered lace pants and a romantic blouse (opposite).

Part of the charm of another gypsy dress by Sant'Angelo was the colorful knit fabric, printed with a variety of exotic patterns to resemble patchwork (see page 58).

and sashes over wildly colorful layered skirts. Sant'Angelo, who was Florentine-born and Argentine-raised, had been discovered by the legendary *Vogue* editor Diana Vreeland after he began experimenting with Lucite jewelry. At her encouragement he turned to designing clothes, which were admired in equal measures for their exuberance and comfort. He loathed zippers, so most of his dresses were constructed without complex fastenings and frequently incorporated easy-to-wear knits for the flexibility and freedom they offered their wearer.[6] *Vogue* featured his extravagant dresses in the March 1969 issue in an article that encouraged viewers to "get a little gypsy spirit stirring."[7] With his *Jane and Cinderella* collection in 1971, Sant'Angelo reworked the gypsy into a tattered princess by slashing the skirts into ribbons. Characteristic of his flair for unusual combinations, one Cinderella dress features stretch knit, pieced in primary colors, with a printed paisley chiffon skirt ripped into long strips for a tattered yet luxe appearance.

Opposite, a gypsy dress by
Sant'Angelo in a lively faux-
patchwork print (1971)

In Sant'Angelo's spring 1971 *Jane
and Cinderella* collection, the
designer revisited the gypsy look,
carefully tearing the skirts into
strips to confer a ravished allure.

The 1967 film *Camelot* helped popularize medieval-style fashions. This advertisement from the same year, trumpeting, "You will feel as proud as Guinevere" in the new Stevetex fabric, shows the rounded neckline, high waist, and flowing pointed sleeves associated with the trend.

A quasi-medieval dress by Lee Bender for Bus Stop, made of sheer silk georgette printed in tones of bright orange and brown, marries the medieval look to a psychedelic floral pattern.

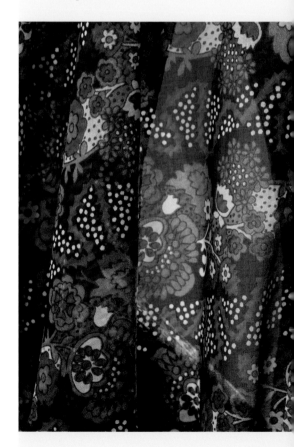

From King Arthur to Queen Elizabeth

The world of knights and ladies was another historical fantasy mined by hippies and designers alike. J. R. R. Tolkien's *Lord of the Rings* was issued for the first time in paperback in 1965, followed not long after by the release of the popular film version of *Camelot*, stimulating an interest in all things medieval, or at least quasi-medieval. Back-to-nature hippies and antiwar activists alike took inspiration from Tolkien's imaginary world of the bucolic, peaceful Shire. Dresses with long, trailing sleeves, round necklines, and skirts with trains were meant to reflect the "medieval" style. *Vogue* ran an advertisement featuring a model wearing a tunic with long flaring sleeves, calling it "the then look of Camelot."[8] Similar sleeves extending into points are a signature feature on a dress designed by Lee Bender for her hip London boutique, Bus Stop.

Renaissance fairs, which flourished in the late 1960s, allowed participants to assume new personas and lead a romanticized historical lifestyle, if only for a brief moment.

An exuberant mélange of medieval and Renaissance
elements was equally appealing to contemporary fashion
designers, who revived techniques such as slashing, cut-
work, and smocking, as well as garments such as shaped
leather jerkins, or jackets, and suede boots. East West
Musical Instruments Company of San Francisco created
imaginative, artful leather clothing in the late 1960s and
1970s, and its Reni (short for Renaissance) suit for men
was one of its most successful designs. Norman Stubbs,
the founder of East West Musical Instruments Company
and designer of the Reni suit, considered the hippie movement itself a renaissance, and therefore found Renaissance
fashion a particularly appropriate inspiration.[9] Made of
buff suede leather, the jacket and trousers feature long
flared cuffs of pieced purple and green suede panels, with
the signature East West floral appliqué decorations. The
overall effect of the Reni suit flamboyantly evokes a jester

Founder Norman Stubbs got the idea for East
West Musical Instruments Company's popular
Reni suit (above, left) from Renaissance
fashions in historical costume books.

This tunic dress by Zandra Rhodes is made
from one of her signature Sparkle prints.
The unconventional shape and cut of a white
version of the tunic was exuberantly captured
in British *Vogue* (March 1971).

or troubadour, making it a favorite among rock stars, like drummer John Bonham of Led Zeppelin, in the late 1960s.

In her 1971 collection, English designer Zandra Rhodes also employed decorative techniques that harked back to Renaissance sources. Her unique dresses were conceived and cut to accommodate her inventive textile designs, often producing dramatic and unusually shaped garments that she dubbed butterflies. In the early 1970s, Rhodes experimented with external seams, pinked edges, and slashed fabrics after seeing Nicholas Hilliard's late-sixteenth-century painted miniatures at the Victoria and Albert Museum. Her Sparkle fabric, part of her *Elizabethan Silks* collection of 1970, was covered in printed ovals, which she then slashed, adding zigzags and hatching that suggested stitching and pinking. She used the textile for both long and short dresses as well as dramatic knee breeches. A black and white version of Sparkle was turned into a short dress with raw edges and traditional hand smocking at the neckline. Rhodes recalled, "For added embellishment, I smocked some of the dresses and from the printed fabric made little silk tassels with pinked raw edges which were held with fine knots of the same material, inspired by Elizabethan stump work."[10]

Romantic Revival

In 1967, just as psychedelic fashions were peaking, *Vogue* announced, "The Romantic look is in the breeze."[11] Seventh Avenue designers such as Oscar de la Renta, Bill Blass, Ferdinando Sarmi, and Geoffrey Beene enthusiastically embraced this revival. In 1971 Blass created an elegant evening dress of black silk organza and taffeta with enormous balloon sleeves and a slightly raised waistline which took direct inspiration from fashions of the Romantic era, circa 1830. Frothy Romantic looks played into Renaissance fantasies, too. In spring 1968 Joseph Thorndike, the editor of *Horizon* magazine, dedicated an issue to the subject of the ubiquitous hippie culture. Like Norman Stubbs, he noted the "resemblance between the Flower People of San Francisco and the Flower People of Renaissance Florence," juxtaposing Sandro Botticelli's masterpiece *Primavera* with an image of a hippie bride.[12] Botticelli's allegory of spring, which embodies

This Bill Blass dress was described as "super romantic" in an article on the appropriateness of black evening dresses in the April 1971 issue of *Vogue*.

Giorgio di Sant'Angelo was likely inspired by Sandro Botticelli's early Renaissance masterpiece *Allegory of Spring* (*La Primavera*) (detail, above) in creating this fantasy dress in sheer printed silk (opposite).

In the early 1970s, British designer Ossie Clark accentuated a Celia Birtwell floral print with a plunging neckline, gathered skirts, full sleeves, and the delicate touch of stitched floral appliqués at the shoulders.

early Renaissance Neoplatonic ideals of love, beauty, and nature, both earthly and spiritual, resonated with back-to-nature adherents. *La Primavera* was likely the inspiration for a dress by Giorgio di Sant'Angelo — a pure flight of fancy in chiffon, printed with colorful blossoms and festooned with three-dimensional silk flowers appliquéd along the gathered sleeves and neckline.

Many designers created dresses that incorporated soft feminine shapes, puffed sleeves, and full skirts without directly quoting recognizable historical styles. Much admired for his chic retro 1930s dresses, Ossie Clark was also brilliant at creating purely romantic confections of sheer fabrics and fluttering silhouettes. Layers of chiffon printed with Celia Birtwell's Pretty Woman floral design make up the flowing skirt of a dress from the early 1970s, gathered just below the deep décolletage, with puffed full sleeves.

Bill Gibb's first solo collection featured textured materials, as in this fur-collared coat made of plush silk printed to look like fur then sumptuously trimmed with real snakeskin. Opposite, actress Meg Wynn Owen strides across the street wearing a very similar Gibb outfit in a photograph from 1972.

Master of Fantasy

Young Scottish designer Bill Gibb's early work for the British clothing manufacturer Baccarat was wildly imaginative, drawing from multifarious sources of fantasy. He quickly gained a reputation for "magpie-like eclecticism" with his combinations of unusual prints and patterned fabrics.[13] His colorful, layered gypsy dresses, described as "glorious confusion" by British *Vogue*, won him the Designer of the Year award in 1970.[14] With this early success under his belt, Gibb launched his own label in 1972, designing a collection inspired by the animal world. Painted leathers, embroidery, knitted tops, beadwork, and feathers figured prominently in the designs. A two-piece ensemble from that first collection was made with silk velvet, cleverly printed and marbleized to mimic animal fur, and trimmed with real lizard skin.

During his brilliant design career, Gibb consistently preferred dramatic shapes inspired by fantasy, drawing on medieval and Renaissance sources as well. In his second collection from spring–summer 1973, he focused on the theme of water, again creating marbleized leathers and pairing them with draped Qiana synthetic knits, flowing capes, scalloped hems, and fabrics printed with shell motifs. A dress from that collection has all the characteristic Gibb fantasy and femininity. Its silhouette is romantic, with a wrap-front closure and puffed batwing sleeves extending into long buttoned cuffs.

The enthusiasm for historical dress among hippies and high-end designers alike was driven in equal measures by nostalgia, fantasy, and a taste for theatricality. It allowed for broad creativity in fashion through role playing and dress-up. These qualities, with their backward glance at the past, could also be seen in a concurrent fashion trend: the revival of art deco and 1940s styles.

A dense printed pattern of seashells in coral and aqua covers the fabric of a dress from Bill Gibb's sea-inspired second collection. The edges are finely overstitched with black and white thread to add visual complexity.

RETRO HIPPIE

French ready-to-wear designer Sonia Rykiel created modern knitwear designs with a retro twist. An ensemble as it appeared in *Vogue* (February 1972) evokes the early 1930s of *Bonnie and Clyde* with its lean lines, long skirt, and beret (above).

This photograph of Karen Seltenrich in a vintage dress appeared on the cover of *Rolling Stone*'s "Groupies" issue in February 1969 (opposite).

While wearers of fantasy fashions searched the remote past for inspiration, some of their peers preferred to travel back in time only a few decades, drawn to the sleek, sophisticated designs of the 1920s, 1930s, and 1940s. Retro adaptations of art deco and wartime fashions delivered an edgier look, with a mixture of camp and panache, in contrast to the romantic nostalgia of medieval, Renaissance, and Edwardian revival styles.

Starting with hippies donning vintage beaded 1920s flapper dresses and shimmering satin 1930s evening gowns, this new take on retro styles evoked the hard-edged glamour of Hollywood rather than the bleaker aspects of the era: the stock market crash of 1929 and the Great Depression. Yet it is no surprise that the youth of the late 1960s, who were themselves in the midst of a cultural revolution, would have been attracted to the late 1920s and early 1930s, which were years of progressive social and political reform, rakishly personified by bootleggers, flappers, and Hollywood vamps. As forgotten American movie classics were revived on television and in college courses and film festivals, they captivated a new generation of fans. The racy sophistication of screen sirens such as Jean Harlow and Carole Lombard inspired young designers' idealized interpretations as they reworked the flowing silhouettes and geometric-patterned fabrics of art deco fashions in their contemporary designs.

Hollywood Glitter

Movies old and new were central to popular conceptions of all things retro. When the trade journal *American Fabrics* announced a new knit fabric called Harlow Cloth, the article proclaimed: "We see Jean crawling across the floor toward an uncaring Clark, all slink and glittering bones, a very suggestive package. Collins & Aikens must have had this in mind, too, when they made Harlow Cloth. It looks like one of the main actors in *The Damned*."[1]

The 1967 release of *Bonnie and Clyde* contributed a different visual nostalgia for the fashions of the interwar years. Starring Warren Beatty and Faye Dunaway, the movie shocked audiences with its vivid portrayal of Clyde Barrow and Bonnie Parker's violent crime spree in the early 1930s. The film's costume designer, Theadora Van Runkle (described by one reporter as wearing clothes from thrift shops in addition to her own designs), acknowledged her debt to hippies and their "freedom of style."[2] Her costumes brought back images of the Depression era in her soft knit ensembles and wool berets for women, and double-breasted tweed suits, fedoras, and oxfords for men. Suits with similar styling—wide lapels, piping, bow ties, cuffed trousers, and large-scale patterned tweeds—were revived by several designers working in this mode in the late 1960s and early 1970s.

(Flower) Power Couple: Celia Birtwell and Ossie Clark

The art deco look could be achieved by wearing actual vintage garments, new fashions by young designers working in a retro style, or a combination of the two. Accessories were a particularly popular way of adding vintage chic to an outfit. *Women's Wear Daily* noted that art deco enamel jewelry and buckles were being "gobbled up" at antique markets in Paris and London by designers and hip "birds."[3] Meanwhile, *Harper's Bazaar* made sure to list the places where its readers could purchase authentic art deco jewelry and handbags.[4] *Rags* featured personalized takes on the style in its pages. A photograph slated for the first issue captured a couple at a late-night deli counter in which the young woman is wearing a 1920s-inspired flapper dress, trailing a contemporary Celia Birtwell chiffon scarf printed with geometric motifs and her signature stylized flowers.

Birtwell, a British textile designer and the creator of iconic floral prints like Mystic Daisy, frequently collaborated with her husband, fashion designer Ossie Clark. Known for his bias-cut moss crepe dresses, Clark designed

Tommy Nutter, a Savile Row–trained tailor, seen here in his own design, was one of the most innovative purveyors of retro men's fashions. Nutter's suits frequently included layered, patterned tweeds, rolled hems, wide lapels trimmed with piping, and flared trousers.

While this young woman (opposite) has chosen a 1920s flapper look, her escort sports a knit shirt topped with a hand-knit vest, bleached blue jeans tucked into knee boots, and a studded belt for an outfit that leans more toward craft hippie than retro hippie.

Made in a cherry-red rayon moss crepe, Ossie Clark's gown from around 1970 features a bias-cut skirt, flaring collar, and long row of fabric-covered buttons extending down the center front well below the waistline.

Celia Birtwell's geometric print appears in this dress's flowing skirt, long pointed double collar, gently flaring sleeves, and shoulder epaulettes (opposite). The fit is classic Ossie Clark — soft and feminine — and the bodice molds itself to the body through his signature bias cutting (1969–70).

sexy, feminine retro looks, incorporating his wife's distinctive printed fabrics. His first important foray into fashion came via fellow Royal College of Art graduate Alice Pollock, who had launched a boutique called Quorum in 1964. Although Birtwell preferred to design and print textiles at home, away from the hectic scene, Clark worked in the offbeat boutique's back room while the beautiful people of London, as well as artist friends like David Hockney, dropped by throughout the day. Even Quorum's van driver was soon to become a star — David Gilmour of Pink Floyd.

Authentic art deco fashions were distinguished by soft draping, extended rounded or pointed collars, elegant flaring sleeves, and geometric prints, worn with small caps or berets. In the early 1930s, fabrics were often cut on the bias to mold to the body, and this technique was revived by several innovative designers including Clark, who was also fond of "old-fashioned" materials — crepes, printed chiffons, glossy satins, and herringbone-patterned woolens. A figure-hugging rayon crepe dress Clark designed in the late 1960s features a bold black and white geometric pattern of triangles and stripes from Birtwell's *Plastic Buildings* collection, which was itself inspired by cubist art. Clark alternated it with a bodice of solid black rayon crepe, artfully pieced in as long triangular inserts. Its drape and cut were conceived for Clark's ideal model — a lean but curvy woman closer in spirit to a 1930s ideal than to the skinny, boyish figure popularized by models of mid-1960s mod fashions.

Pollock and Clark were both highly creative designers but not astute business managers, and in 1968 they invited Alfred Radley, a successful garment manufacturer, to join them as a partner in Quorum. Clark continued to produce his own exclusive lines as Ossie Clark for Quorum, but added a diffusion line called Ossie Clark for Radley. This secondary line translated Clark's original high-end designs into lower-priced garments. A floor-length evening dress designed around 1970 illustrates the high quality maintained in the Radley diffusion line. An elegant and sophisticated reinterpretation of fluid 1930s silhouettes, it became one of Clark's most successful designs.

A champagne satin pantsuit of about 1968 from his own line was dubbed Lamborghini because it evoked the

Ossie Clark's Lamborghini pantsuit in rayon satin from about 1968 (opposite) calls to mind the sleek lines of the classic Italian sports car.

The tight fit, flaring collar, and asymmetrical zipper closure are very modern touches on Ossie Clark's retro-inspired trench coat from about 1969.

automobile's luxury with its figure-hugging shape and shiny fabric. A shimmering tailored jacket complements dramatic trousers in Birtwell's Chinoiserie print, creating a look reminiscent of casual beach pajamas from the 1920s.

Yet Clark could also make garments with a harder edge. The chance procurement of a cache of pristine snakeskins found in a warehouse enabled him to turn out a number of innovative snakeskin garments, including tight-fitting rocker jackets, long coats, and skirts. A calf-length coat from about 1969, one of supposedly only three produced, illustrates Clark's reinterpretation of the classic 1930s trench, as well as his deft manipulation of a difficult material.

Biba

Even with his diffusion line, the majority of Ossie Clark's clothing was not within the means of the average shopper. It was the designer Barbara Hulanicki, with her iconic London boutique, Biba, who brought style to the masses. With its trendy clothes and cheeky attitude, Biba was the place for women seeking the latest trends at affordable prices.

Starting out as a fashion illustrator in the 1950s, Hulanicki turned to designing clothes in the 1960s and launched a limited mail order business called Biba Postal Boutique in 1963. The golden combination of hip style and cheap prices made Biba Postal a success. Even in rural England, Biba customers could access stylish looks through mail order catalogs.

Although the cost of the clothes was within the reach of many, their fit nevertheless made them exclusive to the young and slim. Biba garments were cut with extremely high armholes, narrow shoulders, and tight trousers—shapes best suited to young women in their teens and twenties. And unlike the elegant and feminine look of Ossie Clark's fashions, Biba garments explored the darker, decadent side of art deco. They incorporated vintage elements such as long pointed or rabbit-ear collars, long skirts, wide trouser legs, and narrow jackets with puffed or flaring sleeves, accentuated by period accessories such as feather boas and large floppy hats. The effect was provocative and a bit ambiguous; this knowing parody of nostalgic styles was becoming an increasingly important element

Biba models exude a carefully cultivated aura of youth and sophistication in a woolen pinafore and a trench coat from the pages of the third mail order catalog (1969).

of the fashion dialogue in the early 1970s. Biba's unique look was reinforced by its unusual palette of muddy colors such as mauve, plum, brown, gray, rust, cream, shell pink, and dusty blue. These muted shades provided a sharp contrast to the bright, intense hues of mid-1960s mod and psychedelic fashions. As one Biba shopper later recalled, "These were serious colours and they somehow made Biba catalogs look far more subversive and potentially dangerous than more overtly revolutionary publications."[5]

With the profits from Biba Postal, Hulanicki and her husband and business partner, Stephen Fitz-Simon, were able to shift to selling her clothes in successful retail shops in a series of ever larger spaces, landing on Kensington High Street in 1969. With their dark interiors, potted palms, brass spittoons, and wood paneling, the early shops were vital extensions of the Biba experience. They mirrored the mix of nostalgia and decadence that was at the heart of the Biba look, as art deco styles flirted with Pre-Raphaelite and art nouveau inspirations.

The label's particular type of female beauty was illuminated in its updated mail order catalogs, relaunched in 1968. The covers always featured the iconic fin-de-siècle Biba logo, which was used on everything from women's fashions to makeup, children's clothes, and even menswear, in an early example of branding. Inside the catalog, lean models, usually with curly blond hair and mascara-rimmed eyes, posed in floating dresses. Biba models were young yet exuded a knowing and slightly unearthly quality. They were not the fresh innocents of mid-1960s mod fashions but precocious contemporary youth. With their trancelike gazes and "exaggerated silent movie 'vamp' makeup," argues historian Elizabeth Wilson, "the Biba look could be read as drug culture fashion."[6]

The brand's most public commitment to art deco came with its move to the Big Biba store in 1973. The building, formerly the famous Derry and Toms department store, was a deco gem originally designed in 1933 by architect Bernard George which had fallen into disrepair over the years. Hulanicki and her team lovingly restored the building, including the Rainbow Room restaurant and roof garden. The Biba line expanded, extending beyond fashion to include housewares. By all accounts the Big

Biba store was an extraordinary shopping experience, selling not just products but a lifestyle. Kennedy Fraser, writing for the *New Yorker* in 1974, observed: "The décor—particularly on the main floor and the Rainbow Room restaurant—takes a lot of living up to. The vivid images of Busby Berkeley's sequined choruses fanning out kaleidoscopically from behind Biba's mirrored islands of display, or of Fred Astaire and Miss Rogers whirling down the aisles, conjured up by normally pedestrian journalists at the opening of the new Biba attest to its stimulus.... And it is the only department store in the world daring enough to offer us life, spoof, and romance, too."[7]

The Biba logo, seen here on the cover of a mail order catalogue, was designed by John McConnell as a sophisticated reworking of an art nouveau typeface in black and gold that also suggests Celtic strapwork.

A cheeky nod to 1920s beach pajamas, this early 1970s Biba halter jumpsuit features a geometric art deco print.

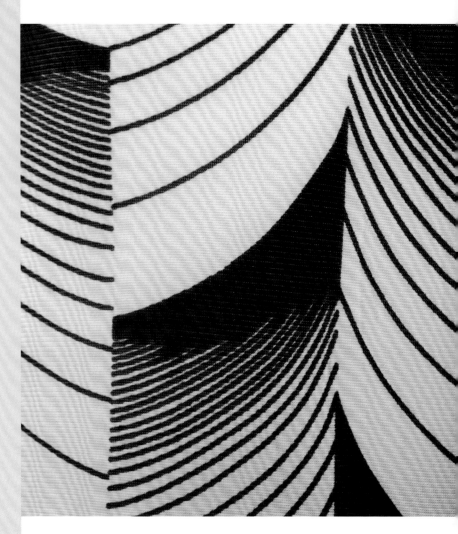

Big Biba's seven stories were painstakingly renovated to evoke the elegant escapism of early 1930s glamour, including mirrored displays, streamlined metalwork, and patterned carpets in signature Biba colors (opposite).

Yves Saint Laurent's 1940s look took the form of knee-length skirts, peplum jackets, wedge shoes, and retro hairstyles, as seen here in an outfit designed for his Rive Gauche line (British *Vogue,* May 1971).

Flirty Forties

Meanwhile, art deco's influence was challenged by another retro style gaining traction at the time — fashions of the 1940s. Knee-length dresses, sweetheart necklines, broad shoulder pads, turbans, and platform wedge shoes began to crop up on the streets and on runways.

Yves Saint Laurent is usually given credit for reviving the 1940s look in high fashion with his notorious fall-winter 1970–71 haute couture *Collection 40,* though he was not the only designer to dabble in that style. *Rags* magazine even went so far as to refer to the collection as "St. Laurent's 'Funny Whore' look (which, like it or not, had already been done by young designers in New York and London)."[8]

Yves Saint Laurent with models wearing his fall–winter 1970–71 haute couture *Collection 40* (about 1971)

This Rive Gauche chubby from the early 1970s is made of blue marabou feathers in place of *Collection 40*'s fur (opposite).

The collection was vilified in the international fashion press. For some French critics, the years of Nazi occupation and collaboration were still too sensitive a subject to be appropriate fodder for fashion. Others objected strictly on aesthetic grounds, simply finding *Collection 40* unattractive. Eugenia Sheppard's review for the *New York Post* called it the "ugliest show in town."[9] The most controversial piece was indisputably the fur jacket, or chubby, as it was known. Made of fox fur dyed bright green, in its full shape and extended shoulder line it not only reminded viewers of the painful war years but also suggested the louche attire of prostitutes. In a review titled "At St. Laurent, Styles for the Demi-Monde," Bernadine Morris declared that "to put another name on it, it's the

Ossie Clark revisited Celia
Birtwell's geometric Plastic
Buildings print, shown here in
an original sketch (opposite),
in a short and sassy 1940s dress
(around 1970).

Detail of Celia Birtwell print
(see previous pages)

Biba's foray into the 1940s look can be
seen in the wide, padded shoulders
of this faux-fur capelet and the sweetheart
neckline of the panne velvet dress
(opposite, early 1970s).

street-walker's 1940s."[10] Despite the critical response, sales
were so successful that St. Laurent created chubbies for
his ready-to-wear line, Rive Gauche, substituting other
materials for the expensive fox fur.

Around the same time that Saint Laurent was creating
Collection 40, Ossie Clark was experimenting with the
1940s look in the form of puffed sleeves, yoke bodices,
and shorter skirts.[11] He also made a 1940s version of his
art deco dress by shortening the skirt to the knee, adding
high, puffed sleeves, a peplum, and a keyhole tie neckline,
while reworking Celia Birtwell's geometric print in yellow
and black.

After successfully mining the darker side of art nouveau and art deco inspiration, Biba was equally enthusiastic in adopting 1940s fashion details for its designs. A
faux-fur wrap with large squared shoulders was one of the
wartime-inspired pieces, which could be worn over dresses
with the signature Biba keyhole or sweetheart neckline or
crepe skirts.

Retro fashions allowed the wearer to experiment with
role playing and fantasy, in this case vicariously experi-
encing the hedonism and sophistication of the art deco
era and the dash of wartime fashions. By self-consciously
looking backward at the vampy glamour of a few decades
earlier, retro styles rejected the fresh-faced futurism of the
mid-1960s mod look and even the fantastical reveries on
a distant past, instead asserting a more subtly shaded take
on campy nostalgia.

ETHNIC HIPPIE

In the 1960s, young people from the United States and Europe were exploring the world in greater numbers than ever before. Whether traveling on their own or through organizations such as the Peace Corps, they roamed the Americas, Africa, Central Asia, and the Middle East, bringing home decorative objects, textiles, and garments. Generalized notions of ethnic or exotic ways of life fueled a growing interest in the luxurious materials found abroad. Silks, velvets, and leathers, embellished with rich embroidery, beads, fringe, gold, and mirrors, contributed to a form of hippie dress marked by vibrant bricolage.

Hippies and rock stars alike gravitated toward the colorful, eclectic duds. Designers and fashion boutiques soon joined in, creating garments based on foreign silhouettes, techniques, motifs, and fabrics. Even Paris couture houses such as Yves Saint Laurent and Lanvin included ethnic details in their haute couture and ready-to-wear collections. Yet commercializing the trend was an especially slippery slope for established designers and manufacturers. Although hippie approximations of ethnic clothing mixed elements from different cultures fairly indiscriminately, high-end versions were immediately seen as false or hypocritical by dint of their association with the Establishment. In an article called "Keeping Up with the Ethnics," *American Fabrics* observed: "Real genuineness is the key. Which means that Seventh Avenue may not be able to climb aboard this trend because the kids don't want Seventh Avenue as a passenger. In fact,

In addition to his extraordinary guitar talent, Jimi Hendrix had an innate sense of style that made him one of the coolest rock musicians of the late 1960s. Here he lounges in a brilliant mélange of Asian textiles and beaded jewelry.

Michael Fish, owner of the Mr. Fish boutique, was renowned for his flamboyant dandy suits, but he also explored ethnic inspirations. His maharajah jacket from about 1970 borrows its shape from Indian garments, but looks to Japanese textiles for the design on the silk, brocaded with gold metallic threads (opposite).

This caftan features colorful embroidery typical of Gujarat, India, and was owned by the American fashion designer Rudi Gernreich about 1970 (below).

In March 1968, the Fab Four assembled in Rishikesh, India, with a large group, including Maharishi Mahesh Yogi and their wives and girlfriends, all in traditional Indian dress (right).

if Seventh Avenue climbs aboard, the kids may climb off. And hunt for something else."[1] Indeed, the ethnic-inspired fashions created by New York, London, and Paris designers became identified as an upscale "rich hippie" look that was flaunted on the Upper East Side of Manhattan, not in the East Village.

Passages to India

In addition to investigating the world outside themselves, young people were drawn to the prospect of interior voyages. In 1968 the Beatles ventured to India to explore Transcendental Meditation with Maharishi Mahesh Yogi, focusing the world's attention on that country's complex culture. Photographs from their visit captured the Beatles wearing various forms of Indian dress, including the *achkan*, a lightweight three-quarter-length coat or tunic distinguished by a short standing collar and often made of richly patterned fabrics. Indian-style clothing became one of the first recognizable ethnic looks to take hold in London, which was quickly consumed by the craze. An article in London's *Sunday Times* listed the achkan among the many manifestations of Indian influence: "Holy man in the Hilton; Sitar in the top ten; Mantra chanting at Speaker's Corner; Achkhan jackets at Hippy weddings. . . ."[2]

The trend became particularly innovative and liberating for menswear as suit and sport coats were transformed into maharajah jackets and collarless Nehru jackets (modeled after the type of jacket worn by Jawaharlal Nehru, India's prime minister in the early 1960s), and traditional cotton and silk tunics took on fanciful avant-garde shapes, colors, and patterns. Designers also offered their own versions of the achkan. Rupert Lycett Green's exclusive men's shop Blades offered a sap-green Nehru suit in Thai silk, while Mr. Fish created a collarless maharajah jacket. For women, traditional forms of Indian dress and decoration were used to conjure an exoticized East. In 1969, New York custom designer Arnold Scaasi used deep red Indian silk fabric brocaded with gold threads to create an evening dress based on a traditional sari.

From Household to Haute Couture

In the late 1960s, fashion magazines frequently featured home interiors lavishly decorated in the new ethnic style. "Baby Jane" Holzer, a former Warhol Factory actress turned society hostess, swathed the dining room of her New York apartment in Indian printed cotton fabrics. The fashion designer Halston, who was later renowned for his ultra-minimalist designs, covered his first Manhattan showroom in floor-to-ceiling faux-batik-printed cottons and "oriental bric-a-brac" to give the impression of a North African souk,[3] and Italian designer Valentino restyled his rooftop apartment in Rome into a Turkish tent.

Meanwhile, British designer Thea Porter opened a boutique in London selling imported Eastern fabrics and rugs, which quickly became a magnet for trendy pop stars and bohemian aristocrats.[4] Born in Jerusalem to missionary parents, she spent her childhood in Damascus, Syria, and her married life in Lebanon, experiences that guided her later selections of furnishing textiles. From her shop on Greek Street in Soho, Porter soon began transforming these exotic imported fabrics into women's "ethnic hippie" garments. A brilliant yellow tie-dyed silk fabric from Gujarat, India, became a peasant dress featuring a low square neckline and romantic puffed sleeves, embellished with traditional embroidery in bands and radiating medallions.

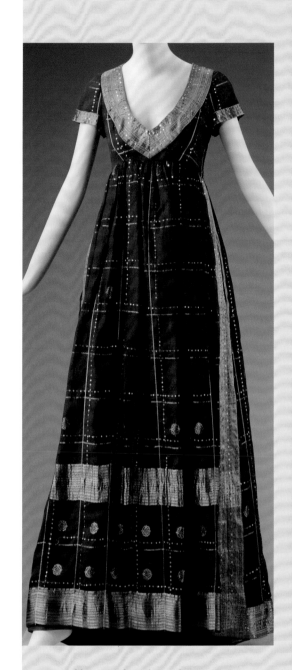

Arnold Scaasi adapted an Indian sari in deep maroon silk brocaded with gold into a fashionable evening dress, worn by Barbra Streisand to the American Diabetes Association Benefit in April 1970.

Yellow silk offers a bright counterpoint to the subtle embroidery from Gujarat, India, that Thea Porter incorporated into a peasant-style dress around 1969 (below). Porter also fashioned a similar textile, but in deep red embellished with sequins, into an upscale caftan trimmed with colorful brocaded floral patches (opposite).

Socialite Jane Holzer wears an embroidered Turkish caftan as she lounges in her dining room upholstered in Indian printed cottons (*Vogue*, November 1969).

Thea Porter took an embroidered Iraqi woolen textile and added an elegant fur collar and cuffs to create a bohemian luxe coat. A slightly different version of the coat appeared in British *Vogue* in November 1970, accessorized with matching boots and bag (opposite).

For another dress, Porter transformed sheer red silk fabric, also from Gujarat, into a long flowing caftan that showcased its tie-dyed pattern of elephants and flowers, gold chain-stitch embroidery with sequins, and patchwork panels of brocaded floral silk.

Building on her penchant for Middle Eastern fabrics, Porter created an extraordinary coat in 1969 using a traditional embroidered textile made by a nomadic people of Iraq. The dense, colorful wool embroidery in the main body of the coat contrasts with a dark fur collar and cuffs for a luxurious look. Interestingly, Porter reused the same geometric pattern seen in the coat's embroidery in a dress, this time printed rather than embroidered. Adding to the rich effect of the dress is its bodice, embellished with bold floral needlework taken from a different source—a traditional embroidery, called a suzani, from Central Asia.

A fragment of a Central Asian floral embroidery, known as a suzani, adorns the bodice of Thea Porter's printed chiffon dress (about 1970).

A long-haired pair at Woodstock keep warm in shaggy wool vests from Afghanistan (1969).

Geoffrey Beene's gypsy dress from 1970 features a large-scale floral pattern set against a crimson silk ground in a vibrant design that looks to Eastern textiles for inspiration.

Central Asian and Middle Eastern Exoticism

Drawn by the unique allure of the clothing worn by the isolated peoples of the great Eurasian steppe, fashion designers trumpeted the "nomad look" in 1969.[5] New York designer Geoffrey Beene, better known for the elegant cut and streamlined design of his clothes, produced a flamboyant peasant dress with fabric printed in a large-scale floral pattern that resonated with the palette and scale of traditional Central Asian textiles.

Garments from Uzbekistan and Afghanistan, especially shaggy sheepskin vests and jackets, were among the earliest ethnic trends for men and frequently appear in photographs of the Beatles, the Rolling Stones, Jimi Hendrix, and other luminaries of the music scene in the late 1960s. The *New York Times* observed that Afghani sheepskins were de rigueur not only for rock stars but for their fans, too. At a Janis Joplin concert in December 1969, the "more daring boys wore such things as black velvet capes, leather maxi coats, and furry Afghanistan-style coats trimmed with colorful embroidery."[6] To meet the growing demand for this trend, new boutiques selling imported goods started to spring up. *Vogue* noted the "Asian invasion" taking place in both London and New York with shops like London's Oxus, "run by two fellows who spell each other touring the East, especially Afghanistan, finding carpets, caftans, lengths of fabric. . . . It's the irresistible urge for the luxury of the East that we all feel."[7]

The same *Vogue* article included a photograph of young New York collector Ira Seret reclining in a swath of antique "purple silk laden with exquisite bullion-embroidery lined in silver fox."[8] Seret is shown wearing a caftan, the long, untailored garment traditionally worn in Muslim countries. Inspired by the North African djellabah (a form of hooded caftan) and Moroccan, Turkish, and Uzbek robes, caftans provided loose, colorful shapes with yards of surface for embellishment.

Talitha and John Paul Getty Jr. relax in bohemian chic Moroccan caftans on the rooftop terrace of their Marrakech home (*Vogue*, January 1970).

English designer John Bates created a luxurious wool crepe djellabah in 1976, featuring a sinuous floral design appliquéd in black silk and embroidered in violet thread. Bates made only two such djellabahs, one of which was owned by *Vogue*'s first London editor, Lady Harlech (née Pamela Colin).

Morocco, in particular, was a popular destination for American and European travelers in the late 1960s, and the caftan's association with the mystique of a secluded culture was part of its allure. Wearers of both genders sported the robes, which designers and boutiques often translated into fashionable evening dresses for women and casual lounging outfits for men. English designer John Bates created a sumptuous woman's djellabah in midnight blue wool embroidered with elegant floral appliqués. The distinguished Savile Row men's tailoring establishment Turnbull & Asser actually imported their embroidered wool caftans from Tangiers, Morocco, while designer Michael Fish created his own updated versions in luxurious fabrics, which were sold through his Mr. Fish boutique in London.

Native American Spirit

Many American designers found inspiration closer to home. In North America, public awareness of and interest in the plight of American Indians had grown through the 1960s, especially with the founding of the American Indian Movement (AIM) in Minnesota in 1968. Fashions both high and low overflowed with a plethora of Native American references, from suede pants and leather jackets to beads, fringe, feathers, forehead bands, boots, and silver jewelry. Committed back-to-nature hippies felt that these accoutrements connected them with a purer way of life and strengthened their spiritual relationship with the land.

Of course, not all fashionable dressers had such idealistic notions. For most, the Native American look was a promiscuous mix of motifs and materials with little thought for accuracy or distinction among the different peoples and tribal arts. It served simply as another interesting dress-up style to sample. And sample it they did. In 1970 *American Fabrics* commented: "The mystique of the American Indian seems to be getting stronger than ever. Fringes, headbands, beaded designs all seem more and more the white man's fashion burden. It started with the hippies, and now walks down 5th Avenue."[9]

Boutiques offering "authentic" American Indian goods proliferated. Some even commissioned Native

American craftspeople to make modern knockoffs of traditional garb. The Ethnics shop in Los Angeles was lauded in *Women's Wear Daily* for taking the lead in creating accurate replicas of American Indian dress and employing three "full-blooded" seamstresses to make "hand woven natural and organic fibers, suede, chiffons, and even upholstery fabrics. Trimmings include bear claws, crow feathers, burnt stems, seeds, lava, porcupine quills, and shells."[10] The *New York Times* reported that another entrepreneur was "keeping Utah's Navajo women busy stringing cedar berries for big-city hippies and fashion devotees who have never seen a mesa."[11]

Giorgio di Sant'Angelo's fall–winter 1970 collection, for which he received the coveted Coty Award, featured a range of dresses in intense colors with ribbon work. A turquoise blue velvet dress from that collection has a prairie hippie silhouette with puffed sleeves and a long skirt, gathered into flounces by colorful woven patterned ribbons that were meant to evoke indigenous ribbon work. The pop star Cher modeled a similar outfit in the August 1970 issue of *Vogue*, where it was given the unfortunate name of the "Squaw dress."[12] More ribbon work appeared on shirts for both men and women sold at the Sidereal Times boutique in Los Angeles, which based its ribbon-trimmed shirts on originals made by Native Americans in Oklahoma. The store was identified in *Vogue*'s boutique column as the favorite shop of Cher and her husband and co-star, Sonny Bono.[13]

The most recognizable and widespread American Indian–inspired fashion was fringed leather, which became an overnight sensation in 1968 and lasted well into the 1970s. *Vogue* reported "Indian-girl fringe pouring down the shoulders" in its "Forecast" column,[14] and Sant'Angelo's 1970 collection featured a two-piece fringed dress, shown in an advertisement for Estée Lauder perfume in *Vogue*, November 1970, on a model with beaded buckskin leggings and braided hair, posed in a room decorated with African masks on the mantel. Fringe's association with the Wild West made it hugely popular for men, appearing on everything from jackets and shirts to pants and even boots. The East West Musical Instruments Company of San Francisco produced one of the most refined

Giorgio di Sant'Angelo crafted a dress for his fall–winter 1970 collection from lush velvet and trimmed it with woven ribbons that evoked the trade items incorporated as decorative elements in the dress of Native American tribes in the late 19th century.

Cher, Lake Powell, Arizona, March 1970.
Photograph by Richard Avedon.

The singer, who claimed some Cherokee
heritage, appeared wearing a Native
American–inspired dress by Giorgio
Sant'Angelo in a photograph published
in *Vogue* in August 1970.

takes on fringed leather with their Swanbone jacket. Made
from drum-dyed top-grain cowhide, the Swanbone sported
deer antler buttons and the signature East West floral
appliqués. According to founder Norman Stubbs, its fringe
was made extra long so that customers could braid or bead
it themselves.[15]

Not only was fringe unisex but it also grew into an
international trend that infiltrated English and French
fashions. London-based Ossie Clark was described in
November 1969 as "kicking up quite a lot of fringe — tier
upon tier of russet suede whirling out and about, laced
tunic, knee-long pants."[16] One of his most inventive and
lively ensembles was a two-piece pantsuit made from
Celia Birtwell's printed yellow silk chiffon and covered
with long fringe. Even Saint Laurent experimented with
the fringed look in his fall–winter 1968 collection. The
New York Times described it as drawing on the American
Indian trend that "New York gobbled up so many months
ago, adding, "The opening number at the Saint Laurent
show is all suede and fringes: a short brown coat, a skirt,
and long trousers. Sometimes the fringe runs down the
sides of the sleeves for a Buffalo Bill Look."[17]

Inca and Aztec Influences

Central and South America also made their way into
the fashion spotlight. In April 1970 *Women's Wear Daily*
observed: "The Inca Indian has inspired a whole collection. When you get down to primitivism, it has nothing
to do with Europe. It is a colorful strain that is definitely
this hemisphere."[18] "This hemisphere" as it may have
been — Sant'Angelo's Coty Award–winning collection for
fall–winter 1970 included several South American details
and dresses — the trend nevertheless managed to cross
the Atlantic. The Paris couture house Nina Ricci, for
one, attempted a distinctly Peruvian look with its 1967
coatdresses.

Other designers evoked the ancient Aztec civilization
of Mexico through fabrics in primary colors and geometric
patterns that also had an impact on Paris fashions. In
1972 the Paris couture house Lanvin created a series of
dresses and coats in bold reds, purples, and yellows that

Nineteen seventy was the year of the poncho, seen above on the streets of Manhattan worn as a skirt.

This Swanbone jacket by East West Musical Instruments Company from about 1968 features a complex pattern of beads worked into an eagle and geometric shapes (opposite). East West jackets were also known for the "stash" pockets sewn into neckbands, which offered a convenient hiding place for illegal substances.

the designer called Aztec. Mexican associations, however, were most apparent in the craze for ponchos in the late 1960s and early 1970s. *Women's Wear Daily* reported: "The poncho is everywhere . . . from the stuffiest corners of the arrondissement to the Latin Quarter. The boutiques on the Left have hand-crocheted ones in every color under the Aztec sun. . . . The French girls like their ponchos any way — knitted, crocheted, patterned, plain . . . over pants, or short skirts."[19] In New York, ponchos were frequently worn as skirts, valued for their "simplicity, honesty, and direct-ness" in creating "a Mexican hand-crafted look."[20] This handcrafted quality had become increasingly valued in the late 1960s and early 1970s. An extension of the hippie rejection of all things plastic or mass-produced, handmade and hand-embellished fashions proliferated alongside a revival of traditional crafts from cultures across the globe.

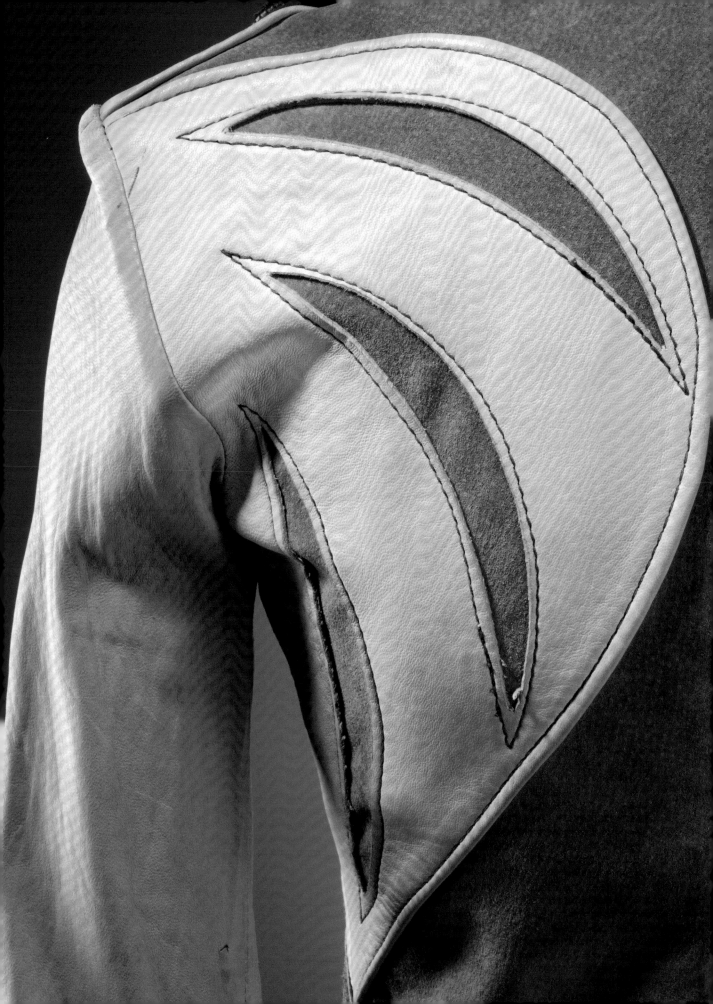

CRAFT HIPPIE

Making, rather than buying, fashion was a hall-mark of the hippie lifestyle. Handmade clothing represented a rejection of consumerism and a response to the counterculture call for self-sufficiency while also allowing room for personal expression. Interest in reviving crafts was not new. In the postwar years the studio craft movement, spearheaded by a younger generation of artists in the United States, had drawn on traditional techniques, combining them with unconventional materials in new, expressive ways. By the late 1960s, appreciation of hand-crafted ceramics, glass, furniture, and textiles had moved beyond artistic circles to the general public. In a decade that witnessed an explosion in technological innovations and methods of mass production, as well as the prolifera-tion of synthetic materials, many crafts that were revived in the late 1960s possessed a unique and fresh charm.

Back-to-nature hippies were keen on making their own food, shelter, and clothing, delighting in the creative effects that could be achieved through embroidery, patchwork, tie-dye, and painting. Guides including the influential *Whole Earth Catalog* and craft manuals also helped make batik, quilting, macramé, knitting, crochet, and leather tooling immensely popular. The urge to make artful clothes with unconventional techniques found expression in boutique fashions and trickled upward into Paris haute couture, which had its own history of luxury craftsmanship. Traditional fashion designers responded to populist handicraft trends by incorporating, distilling, and honing elements of craft in their own highly refined ways.

Gloria Vanderbilt was one of many New York socialites to embrace the patchwork craze, turning old quilts into garments and furnishing fabrics. She is shown wearing a patchwork dress in her bedroom, which she'd redecorated with panels of patchwork (*Vogue*, February 1970).

123

Tie-Dye

With its swirling, colorful patterns formed by knotting or binding and then dyeing cloth, tie-dye was closely associated with psychedelic fashions as well as ethnic styles. The technique itself is an ancient one; it can be found in the traditional arts of Indian *bandhani*, West African *adire oniko*, Japanese *shibori*, and Indonesian *ikat*. It was cheap and easy to do at home, and hippies tie-dyed everything from T-shirts to upholstery. *Vogue* encouraged its readers: "Knot it. Squinch it. Dip it in the dye pot. Wring it out. The more uneven the color the better it is."[1]

Tie-dye attracted craft artists and young fashion designers as well as enthusiastic amateurs. The designs of Ann Thomas, who founded Water Baby Dye Works in San Francisco, were featured in *Rags* magazine. Marijke Koger and Simon Posthuma (formerly of the psychedelic artist collective The Fool) tie-dyed and airbrushed fabric to create colorful clothing and accessories into the 1970s. And through her boutique in Hollywood, designer Holly Harp sold her own artful tie-dyed dresses to the likes of Linda Ronstadt, a reigning queen of rock.

Designer Holly Harp started out reworking vintage fashions before moving on to hand-painted and tie-dyed silks, which she sold from her shop on the Sunset Strip. In this dress, a tie-dyed silk skirt with handkerchief hemline, richly patterned bodice, and suede corset-belt combine to create a sexy yet carefully crafted gypsy look.

Opposite, the blue sky and exotic tile work of the shrine of Harun-i Vilayat in Isfahan, Iran, complement Halston's sumptuous panne velvet robe, tie-dyed in blue, white, and green (*Vogue*, December 1969). Halston became enamored with tie-dye in the late 1960s and patronized several different artists. His pantsuit boasts a richly tie-dyed silk velvet created by artists Will and Eileen Richardson of Up-Tied (right).

Halston's 1969–70 collection featured silks colored by artists Will and Eileen Richardson of Up-Tied, who were considered the best tie-dyers in New York City. Halston's tie-dye designs appeared frequently in both *Harper's Bazaar* and *Vogue* in 1969. One of his most sensuous pieces was a silk velvet pantsuit dyed in colorful splotches of yellows and greens, from his 1969 fall–winter collection. Asked about his interest in tie-dye, the designer explained, "The beauty of it is that no two pieces are alike, and anybody can wear it—young and not so young."[2] Halston's clientele included both camps, from Liza Minnelli to socialite Babe Paley, glamorous and well-heeled trendsetters seeking the "rich hippie" look. Even luxurious fashion items like high-end furs were not immune; *Vogue* heralded the "fireworks of colour, pattern, and design" on a "brilliant tie-dye mink cape" designed by Georges Kaplan.[3]

Patchwork

Like tie-dye, patchwork was a humble handicraft enthusiastically adopted by hippies, then taken up by the wider populace. Traditionally patchwork was employed to extend the life of ripped, tired clothes, a form of recycling that accorded with hippie frugality. Yet the impetus behind patching clothes in the late 1960s and early 1970s had little to do with the need to mend or make do. The time-intensive process of hand stitching was instead used to transform plain garments into elaborate and truly luxurious pieces of wearable collage. By 1971 *Time* magazine was reflecting: "Long ago—perhaps as far back as the early 1960s—patches on worn or torn clothing were a mark of poverty, or at least thrift. The patchwork has come a long way since then. Today, it is colorful, clever, artistic, and even ideological."[4]

Patchwork was integral to the creations of several young, hip fashion designers. In London, Granny Takes a Trip offered a psychedelic boot with gold or silver stars on blue leather, while over on Savile Row, innovative menswear designer Tommy Nutter was creating suits and separates from a patchwork of suiting woolens. Boutiques, in turn, began to sell garments made from antique quilts.

At Granny Takes a Trip, around 1969, you could custom order an "astrology patched boot" by Gohill shoemakers for about $55.

Hippies had introduced the look by turning old patchwork quilts into skirts or jackets, but in 1969 *Vogue* reported that at Serendipity 3 in New York one could find "the real thing, an antique silk and velvet patchwork quilt cut up into a cardigan and culottes" for $200.[5]

New York's social elite took up the trend too. In March 1969 *Women's Wear Daily* reported: "Now the ladies like Gloria Vanderbilt Cooper, Jackie O, Barbara Hutton, Marie-Pierre de Cicco, and Teresa Heinz are all bringing in their old patchwork comforters and quilts, most bought at antique shops. They've taken them off their beds and are having Adolfo whip them up into evening skirts.

Andrée Brossin de Méré in Paris created a rich patchwork of colored silks, satins, and velvets for this Yves Saint Laurent dress, which appeared in *L'Officiel* in September 1969 (opposite).

Italian designers Ottavio and Rosita Missoni established a booming business creating colorful and innovative knit garments like this 1972 three-piece outfit with an exuberant pattern of waves and circles in red, green, and blue.

Opposite, crochet goes upscale in a dress designed by Paris couturier Louis Féraud (*Vogue*, November 1969).

Sometimes they put a gingham apron over them for a peasant look.... Other times they mix pattern with pattern by adding a striped or gingham shirt and tie it all together with a striped ribbon for effect."[6] The Fifth Avenue department stores B. Altman and Henri Bendel began marketing patchwork garments created by several new cooperatives, such as Patch Blossom and Mountain Artisans, which had been established to assist artists in rural Appalachia. One such skirt was described in the *New York Times* as "the work of a 91 year old widow, one of the oldest and most skilled of the two hundred white and black women who work in the Patch Blossom cottage industry program that is being formed into a cooperative based in Tazewell, VA."[7]

The ultimate faux-poverty fashion statement was made by Yves Saint Laurent. Keenly aware of street and boutique trends, Saint Laurent created several patchwork dresses for his 1969 haute couture collections. One of the most luxurious was an evening dress from the fall–winter collection. It contained more than two hundred pieces of printed silk and velvet, artfully stitched into a dazzling mosaic by the venerable house of Mme. Andrée Brossin de Méré in Paris. This was patchwork at its most rarefied and most expensive.

Needles and Thread

By 1969, needlework of all types had become chic. In the spirit of hippie creativity and individuality, *Rags* magazine urged its readers, both men and women, to take up free-form knitting: "It's new Knit! ... An abstract expressionist painting that you wear. An opportunity to invent a new definition for the word clothes. Everybody is a star, no two alike, for next to no money. Make something for a friend that can't be found in stores."[8]

While anyone with knitting needles and a bit of patience could whip up a poncho, it was the young Italian designers Ottavio and Rosita Missoni who successfully reinterpreted knitting for the ready-to-wear market. Together they designed sophisticated knitted ensembles, distinguished by bold patterns and vivid colors, as well as imaginative layered looks.

Crochet, popular in the Victorian period, was even

easier than knitting, employing only a single hooked needle. The technique made quick work of vests, shawls, skirts, and caps with a hippie feel. A wide range of designers from Halston to Louis Féraud incorporated crochet into their ready-to-wear collections.[9]

Macramé was for the most part a lost craft until artist Virginia Harvey's influential publication *Macramé: The Art of Creative Knotting* catapulted it into the public consciousness in 1967. It required no special tools, just yarn or string fixed to a mount to allow successive knotting of the threads to form as simple or complex a web as the maker desired. Macramé became a household word, as well as a ubiquitous decorative element in homes. Macramé belts, headbands, plant holders, and wall hangings, especially those incorporating organic materials such as feathers and stones, had become part of the popular culture by 1970 and were made by young and old alike. *American Fabrics* called the nostalgic craze "further demonstration of the turn to handicrafts in a machine age."[10]

Leather

The hippies' rejection of mass-produced and synthetic materials, as well as their interest in indigenous cultures, fed into the revival of leather craft. Leather made a solid yet supple base for tooled, painted, braided, fringed, and pieced-inlay designs. Jackets and skirts made from animal skins proliferated, and accessories were equally popular. In 1970 *Women's Wear Daily* could report: "Leather and suede are the jewelry materials of today. Young designers who go for the softer look in jewelry use leather for necklaces, bracelets, earrings, and belts. They mix it up with wood, beads, and metal."[11]

Hippies interested in personalizing their clothes painted old leather garments to give them new life. The designer Charlotte de Vazquez took this a step further when she moved to Mexico and started a leather fashion company under the label Char. Her garments and accessories featured pieced and appliquéd leather, frequently painted with floral and animal designs by artists of Tonalá in Guadalajara, Mexico. The garments were cut out of dyed calfskin in Char's workshops at Las Fuentes, then stitched

The delicate floral and bird motifs on the panels of a Char vest from about 1970 are typical of the style of Andrés Mera, a Mexican artist who painted many Char leather garments.

Char created this luxurious long patchwork vest by stitching together suede and hand-painted leather panels (opposite).

In the East West Musical Instruments Company's Parrot jacket from about 1970, multicolored suede and leather appliqués are cleverly arranged to create the impression of a bird's head and wings.

and laced together by local women. After assembly, they were passed on to the artists, most of whom were also connected with the local ceramic industry. According to Vazquez, painting had to be done by daylight, since most villagers' homes had no electricity. One of Char's finest designs — a patchwork leather vest — features elaborate painting by Andrés Mera, who also worked in the local pottery workshops.

Leather inlay was the specialty of Mirandi Babitz and Clem Floyd, who opened their own shop on the Sunset Strip in Los Angeles in 1968. Located just six blocks from the Whisky a Go Go club, and next door to the Psychedelic Conspiracy head shop, Mirandi Leather more often than not had a chain with a "Closed" sign drawn across its front door. Customers knew how to contact Mirandi and Clem (they lived illegally in the back of the shop). They were mostly musicians in the thriving Los Angeles rock scene, including David Crosby of Crosby, Stills & Nash, Paul Kantner of Jefferson Airplane, and John Kay of Steppenwolf. One of their clients was particularly obsessed with achieving the right look for his black leather trousers — Jim Morrison of the Doors.

Mirandi and Clem specialized in one-of-a-kind clothing, which was often historically inspired, embellished with contrasting inlays in floral or animal shapes. They had started out in London by ransacking flea markets for prototypes, then progressed to more innovative and fantastical designs. This blending of imagination with traditional methods and hand tools defined fashion in the late 1960s and early 1970s, according to Clem, and fueled their own design work with leather.[12]

The source of a popular line of western fringed garments, the East West Musical Instruments Company of San Francisco likewise produced some of the most extraordinary leather garments of the era. East West was the brainchild of Norman Stubbs, who founded it in 1967 to market a leather string instrument, similar to a sitar, which he had designed. After limited success with the instrument, Stubbs turned to making pieced, appliquéd, and dyed leather jackets with highly imaginative designs.

East West Musical Instruments Company was unconventional in its business model as well. An experiment

in hippie capitalism and management, it maintained a rotating four-days-on, two-days-off workweek to allow its employees, most of whom were in their twenties, more flexibility. A wall of vinyl records eight feet high fed the constant flow of rock music in the workrooms, and workers enjoyed more joint breaks than coffee breaks, as well as the freedom to take off if the urge to travel hit. A floating pool of employees cycled in and out of East West until its demise in 1979, and former employees were always welcomed back. As Stubbs recalled, "We respected their journey."[13]

Stubbs's organic approach to design can be seen in two of the most original jackets produced by East West, the Janti and the Parrot. He integrated hand-painted cartouches into the Janti jacket (a twist on the word "jaunty") along with his signature floral appliqués. Whether painted by artist David Warren or airbrushed by Steven Rebuck, the cameos depicted the color and foliage of the Seven Sacred Pools in Maui, Hawaii, Stubbs's home state.

Preferring to "construct in the mind," Stubbs began the design of the Parrot jacket not with a sketch but with a question: "How can I make a jacket look like a bird?"[14] He found the answer in a trompe l'oeuil transformation of the collar into parrot heads and beaks, with the birds' plumage suggested through colorful appliqués extending down the jacket.

An example of wearable art, the Parrot jacket proclaims the importance placed on creative fashions in the late 1960s and early 1970s. The revival of traditional crafts brought artful and original handmade garments within the reach of the public, not just patrons of Paris haute couture fashion, and their popularity would last well after the hippie era ended.

East West Musical Instruments Company employees model the Parrot jacket for women and the Janti jacket for men in a marketing photograph from the early 1970s.

Epilogue

After hippie style trickled up from the streets to inform high fashion's rich hippie look, it trickled right back down, influencing mainstream clothing. Mass production sounded the death knell for hippie chic fashions. Once the mainstream tuned in, the fashionable avant-garde dropped out, moving on in its pursuit of the latest edgy trends. High-end designers quickly decamped as well. By 1972 the *New York Times* was already reporting that "the peacock has tucked in its tail feathers," as menswear took a more conservative turn. "The cascading scarves are gone, and so are the trailing fringes, enormous belts, electric colors, and giant window pane plaid suits."[1] This shift was echoed in women's wear. "The fashion revolution is winding down," declared *Times* critic Bernadine Morris in her review of fall fashions for 1972.[2]

Nevertheless, the parade of troubadours, gypsies, and groupies left an indelible mark that amounted to more than the sum of its eclectic parts. As Joseph Thorndike astutely predicted in *Horizon* magazine as early as 1968: "The Hippie cult itself, with its beads and drugs and outlandish clothes, may soon flower and die. But it will not leave our civilization unchanged."[3] Hippies altered the way people related to their clothes, inviting rule breaking and the confounding of expectations. As clothing became a reflection of personality, politics, and lifestyle, it suddenly provided a space to experiment freely, regardless of the dictates of Paris. This mandate for personal expression would be realized in many subsequent trends.

As the 1970s progressed, fashion would become multifarious, defined by no one style but by many. Streamlined soft knits, ideally suited to the disco dance floor, would be the hallmark of designers such as Halston, Jean Muir, and Sonia Rykiel, while others, including Giorgio Armani and Yves Saint Laurent, embraced more tailored looks.

Some even worked in more than one style at once: the ultimate chameleon, Karl Lagerfeld, created highly original and distinctive fashions that drew from trends on opposite sides of the spectrum for each of his labels. The 1970s also witnessed the emergence of a new street style in London. Called punk, it communicated its angry message of protest through ripped jeans, bondage trousers, safety pins, and Doc Marten boots instead of flower power. Yet the anarchic punk, like new wave, goth, and grunge after it, would never have flourished if the hippies hadn't paved the way with their own rebellious style.

Today we also participate in the hippie legacy as we dabble freely in different looks, old and new, echoing the fun of the hippie dress-up box. In the age of the Internet, fashion mavericks create virtual boutiques online, descendants of the quirky shops that once dotted city streets, which reach fans and customers on screens around the globe. The interactive attitude fostered by hippies four decades ago has been taken up by a whole new world of bloggers and street-style photographers who eagerly share what they see and comment on how they see it, creating fashion tribes of their own—and high-end designers continue to draw inspiration from the street. The spirit of hippie chic lives on.

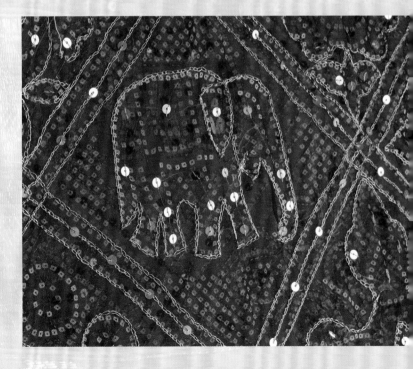

Notes

Hippie Chic:
From the Street to the Runway

1. Ted Polhemus, *Streetstyle* (London: Thames and Hudson, 1994), 66.
2. J. H. Plumb, "The Secular Heretics," *Horizon* 10, no. 2 (Spring 1968): 11.
3. For an excellent overview of the hippie movement, see Barry Miles, *Hippie* (London: Essential Works, 2005), 9.
4. Betsey Johnson, interview with the author, April 11, 2012.
5. Jon Carroll, "A Rags Special Report: Boutiques and Hip Capitalism," *Rags*, February 1971, 42.
6. Jennie Dearden quoted in Judith Watt, *Ossie Clark, 1965–1974* (London: V&A Publications, 2003), 65.
7. Tom Wolfe, *The Electric Kool-Aid Acid Test* (New York: Farrar, Straus & Giroux, 1968), 391.
8. Blair Sabol, "Do You Believe in Magic?" *Rags*, March 1971, 22.
9. Blair Sabol, "Rock Threads," *Show*, March 1970, 31.
10. Kaffe Fassett quoted in Iain R. Webb, *Bill Gibb: Fashion and Fantasy* (London: V&A Publishing, 2008), 10.
11. Marilyn Bender, "The Fashion Decade: As Hems Rose, Barriers Fell," *New York Times*, December 9, 1969.

Trippy Hippie

1. Paul McCartney quoted in Norman Hathaway and Dan Nadel, *Electrical Banana: Masters of Psychedelic Art* (Bologna: Damiani, 2011), 5.
2. From a short British Pathé film, "Beatles' Apple Boutique Opens." http://www.britishpathe.com/video /beatles-boutique-aka-beatles-apple -boutique-opens/
3. Barbara Birdfeather, "Cosmic Couture," *Rags*, March 1971, 59.
4. Nigel Waymouth quoted in Marnie Fogg, *Boutique: A '60s Cultural Phenomenon* (London: Mitchell Beazley, 2003), 175.

5. John Pearse quoted in Max Décharné, *King's Road: The Rise and Fall of the Hippest Street in the World* (London: Orion Books, 2006), 182.
6. John Pearse, e-mail message to the author, July 22, 2009.
7. Décharné, *King's Road*, 182.

Fantasy Hippie

1. Alexa Davis, "Old Clothes: Never Trust Anything under 30," *Rags*, January 1971, 43.
2. Nic Cohn quoted in Marnie Fogg, *Boutique: A '60s Cultural Phenomenon* (London: Mitchell Beazley, 2003), 70.
3. Bernadine Morris, "Taffeta and Lace: Return of an Old, Romantic Look," *New York Times*, November 4, 1969.
4. "Chintz back in Fashion," *Women's Wear Daily*, September 8, 1970, 46; "Romantic Challis Returns," *American Fabrics*, Spring–Summer 1971, 10.
5. "Pretty Is the Word for Cotton," *Vogue*, November 15, 1967, 116.
6. David Colman, "Wild Child," *New York Magazine*, February 18, 2002, http:// nymag.com/shopping/articles/02 /springfashion/santangelo.htm.
7. "Getting It All Together . . . the New Inventiveness in Fashion Starring Jean Shrimpton," *Vogue*, March 15, 1969, 56.
8. Advertisement, *Vogue*, November 1, 1967, 71. Camelot, of course, had a special nostalgic resonance as a metaphor for the glamorous Kennedy administration, which had come to such a tragic end only a few years before.
9. Norman Stubbs, interview with the author, April 5, 2012.
10. Zandra Rhodes and Anne Knight, *The Art of Zandra Rhodes* (Boston: Houghton Mifflin, 1985), 71.
11. "Preview," *Vogue*, July 1967, 45.
12. Joseph J. Thorndike, "Flower People Then and Now," *Horizon* 10, no. 2 (Spring 1968): 2.
13. Iain R. Webb, *Bill Gibb: Fashion and*

Fantasy (London: V&A Publishing, 2008), 10.
14. Ibid., 8.

Retro Hippie

1. "Directions: The Thirties; Harlow Cloth Suggests Thirties," *American Fabrics*, Spring 1970, 8.
2. Enid Nemy, "A Free Spirit Battles Puritanism Despite Chill," *New York Times*, January 17, 1968.
3. "Art Deco — The Now Inspiration for Fashion," *Women's Wear Daily*, April 3, 1969, 1; "Art Deco," *Women's Wear Daily*, April 8, 1969, 4.
4. "Bazaar's Bazaar," *Harper's Bazaar*, September 1969, 272.
5. Catherine Ross, "Biba, Black Dwarf, Black Magic Women," in *Biba: The Label, the Lifestyle, the Look* (Newcastle: Tyne and Wear Museums, 1993), 13.
6. Ibid., 9.
7. Kennedy Fraser, *The Fashionable Mind: Reflections on Fashion, 1970–1981* (New York: Alfred A. Knopf, 1981), 107.
8. "Cop Out on Couture," *Rags*, September 1970, 60.
9. Eugenia Sheppard, "The Ugliest Show in Town," *New York Post*, February 1, 1971.
10. Bernadine Morris, "At St. Laurent, Styles for the Demi-Monde," *New York Herald Tribune*, January 29, 1971.
11. See "Best New Ideas to Walk Away With," British *Vogue*, September 1, 1971, 95.

Ethnic Hippie

1. "Keeping Up with the Ethnics," *American Fabrics*, Winter 1971, 45.
2. Elizabeth Good and Brigid Keenan, "Indian Summer," *Sunday Times* (London), September 3, 1967.
3. Elaine Gross and Fred Rottman, *Halston: An American Original* (New York: HarperCollins, 1999), 8.

4. See *Vogue*, January 15, 1969, 200.

5. See "The Nomad Look," *Harper's Bazaar*, August 1968, 122–35.

6. Judy Klemesrud, "Rock Fans Play Fashion Game, Too," *New York Times*, December 26, 1969.

7. "The Asian Invasion," *Vogue*, August 15, 1970, 133.

8. Ibid.

9. "American Indian Mystique," *American Fabrics*, Fall 1970, 12.

10. "Something Old, Something New: That's the LA Boutique Scene These Days," *Women's Wear Daily*, March 11, 1969, 18.

11. "Squirrels, Beads, and the Hippie-Bead Fad Give Navajos a Lift," *New York Times*, September 7, 1968.

12. "Chér-okee in Panne Velvet and Suede," *Vogue*, August 15, 1970, 79.

13. "Vogue's Own Boutique," *Vogue*, August 15, 1967, 168.

14. "Forecast," *Vogue*, January 1, 1970, 118.

15. Norman Stubbs, e-mail message to the author, June 30, 2012.

16. "Jane Birkin's Got What It Takes — London Snap, Paris Dash," *Vogue*, November 1, 1969, 197.

17. Gloria Emerson, "Buffalo Bill Look Rides High in Paris," *New York Times*, July 30, 1969.

18. "Blue Inca," *Women's Wear Daily*, April 17, 1970, 1.

19. "September Is Comeback Time in Paris," *Women's Wear Daily*, September 30, 1969, 27.

20. "Directions #16," *American Fabrics*, Spring–Summer 1971, 8.

Craft Hippie

1. "*Vogue*'s Own Boutique," *Vogue*, October 15, 1969, 153.

2. "Modern Living: The Psychedelic Tie-Dye Look," *Time*, January 26, 1970, http://www.time.com/time/magazine/article/0,9171,878729,00.html.

3. "The New Furs — Colourific!" *Vogue*, August 15, 1970, 88.

4. "Patchwork Fashions," *Time* 98, no. 2, July 12, 1971, 58.

5. "Patchwork . . . Patchwork," *Vogue*, June 1969, 155.

6. "The Patchwork Peasants," *Women's Wear Daily*, March 26, 1969, 4.

7. Rita Reif, "They Call Their Line Patch Blossom," *New York Times*, July 24, 1971.

8. Uhshur P. Quietstone, "New Knit for Non-Knitters," *Rags*, September 1970, 22.

9. For examples of designer crochet, see "Lauren Hutton — Hooked on Crochet," *Vogue*, January 15, 1970, 162–65, and "From Paris: Louis Féraud's Bright Wool Peasantries . . ." *Vogue*, November 1, 1969, 208.

10. "Enka Gets Into Macramé Boom with New Rayon Satin Cord," *American Fabrics*, Winter 1971–72, 95.

11. "Leather Workings," *Women's Wear Daily*, March 13, 1970, 20.

12. Clem Floyd (Ron Atlee), interview with the author, July 27, 2012.

13. Norman Stubbs, interview with the author, April 5, 2012.

14. Ibid.

Epilogue

1. The Associated Press, "Men's Fashion: A Return to Elegance," *New York Times*, February 5, 1972. See also Angela Taylor, "Peacock Pulling in Its Feathers," *New York Times*, March 11, 1972, and Bernadine Morris, "Fashion's Mood for Fall: Back to Normal," *New York Times*, April 6, 1972.

2. Bernadine Morris, "Fashions: They'll Be Quieter, but That Doesn't Mean Dull," *New York Times*, April 30, 1972.

3. Joseph J. Thorndike, *Horizon* 10, no. 2 (Spring 1968): 6.

Further Reading

Biba: The Label, the Life Style, the Look. Newcastle upon Tyne: Tyne and Wear Museums, 1993.

Birtwell, Celia, and Dominic Lutyens. *Celia Birtwell.* New York: St. Martin's, 2011.

Bluttal, Steven, ed. *Halston.* London: Phaidon, 2001.

Breward, Christopher, David Gilbert, and Jenny Lister, eds. *Swinging Sixties: Fashion in London and Beyond, 1955–1970.* London: V&A Publishing, 2006.

Costantino, Maria. *Men's Fashion in the Twentieth Century: From Frock Coats to Intelligent Fibers.* New York: Costume and Fashion Press, 1997.

Décharné, Max. *King's Road: The Rise and Fall of the Hippest Street in the World.* London: Phoenix, 2006.

Fogg, Marnie. *Boutique: A '60s Cultural Phenomenon.* London: Mitchell Beazley, 2003.

Fraser, Kennedy. *The Fashionable Mind: Reflections on Fashion, 1970–1981.* New York: Knopf, 1981.

Gorman, Paul. *The Look: Adventures in Rock and Pop Fashion.* London: Adelita, 2006.

Gross, Elaine, and Fred Rottman. *Halston: An American Original.* New York: HarperCollins, 1999.

Grunenberg, Christoph, and Jonathan Harris, eds. *Summer of Love: Psychedelic Art, Social Crisis and Counterculture in the 1960s.* Liverpool: Liverpool University Press, 2005.

Healy, Robyn. *Couture to Chaos: Fashion from the 1960's to Now.* Victoria, Australia: The National Gallery of Victoria, 1996.

Hathaway, Norman, and Daniel Nadel. *Electrical Banana: The Masters of Psychedelic Art.* Bologna, Italy: Daminani, 2012.

Hulanicki, Barbara: *From A to Biba.* London: Hutchinson, 1983.

Jacopetti, Alexandra, and Jerry Wainwright. *Native Funk and Flash: An Emerging Folk Art.* San Francisco: Scrimshaw, 1974.

Lester, Richard, and Marit Allen. *John Bates: Fashion Designer.* Woodbridge, Suffolk, England: Antique Collectors Club, 2008.

Leventon, Melissa. *Artwear: Fashion and Anti-Fashion.* New York: Thames and Hudson, 2005.

Lobenthal, Joel. *Radical Rags: Fashions of the Sixties.* New York: Abbeville, 1990.

Meek, Jan, ed. *Yves Saint Laurent: Retrospective.* Sydney: The Art Gallery of New South Wales, 1987.

Miles, Barry. *Hippie.* London: Cassell Illustrated, 2004.

Milinaire, Caterine, and Carol Troy. *Cheap Chic.* New York: Harmony Books, 1975.

Morris, Bernadine, and Barbra Walz. *The Fashion Makers: An Inside Look at America's Leading Designers.* New York: Random House, 1978.

Polhemus, Ted. *Street Style: From Sidewalk to Catwalk.* London: Thames and Hudson, 1994.

Rhodes, Zandra, and Anne Knight. *The Art of Zandra Rhodes.* Boston: Houghton Mifflin, 1985.

Ross, Geoffrey Aquilina. *The Day of the Peacock: Style for Men, 1963–1973.* London: V&A Publishing, 2011.

Savignon, Jéromine, Gilles de Bure, and Pierre Bergé. *Saint Laurent Rive Gauche: Fashion Revolution.* New York: Abrams, 2012.

Watson, Linda. *Ossie Clark: Fashion Designer, 1942–1996.* Warrington, England: Warrington Museum and Art Gallery, 1999.

Watt, Judith. *Ossie Clark, 1967–1974.* London: V&A Publishing, 2003.

Webb, Iain R. *Bill Gibb: Fashion and Fantasy.* London: V&A Publishing, 2008.

Welters, Linda. "The Natural Look: American Style in the 1970's." *Fashion Theory: The Journal of the Dress* 12, no. 4 (2008): 489–510.

Checklist

Unless otherwise stated, all objects are from the collection of the Museum of Fine Arts, Boston. Garment dimensions represent center back measurement.

PAGE 28

Woman's jacket
Retailed at Alkasura
(English, active 1967–1975)
England (London), about 1970
Printed acetate twill weave
70 cm (27 9/16 in.)
Arthur Tracy Cabot Fund 2010.664

PAGE 29

Dress
Designed by Thea Porter
(English, born in Jerusalem, 1927–2000)
England (London), early 1970s
Printed silk plain weave (chiffon)
129.5 cm (51 in.)
Loan Courtesy of the FIDM Museum
at the Fashion Institute of Design
& Merchandising, Los Angeles
Gift of the Fashion Institute of Design &
Merchandising

PAGES 30–31

Woman's evening ensemble
Designed by Hanae Mori
(Japanese, born in 1926)
Japan, 1968–1970
Printed silk plain weave (chiffon)
Romper: 153.3 cm (53 1/4 in.); shawl:
91.4 x 315 cm (36 x 124 in.)
Loan Courtesy of the FIDM Museum
at the Fashion Institute of Design
& Merchandising, Los Angeles
Gift of Anonymous Donor

PAGES 34–35

Tunic dress
Designed by Yosha Leeger (Dutch, worked
in America, 1943–1991) for The Chariot
Cosmic Couture (American, active
1970–1980s)
United States (Los Angeles), about 1970
Hand-printed cotton velvet
82.6 cm (32 1/2 in.)
Museum purchase with funds donated by
the Fashion Council, Museum of Fine Arts,
Boston 2009.329

PAGES 36–37

Man's suit
Retailed at Granny Takes a Trip
(English, active 1966–1974)
England (London), about 1969
Rayon velvet with acetate lining
Jacket: 78.1 cm (30 3/4 in.); waistcoat: 58.4 cm
(23 in.); pants: 106 cm (41 3/4 in.)
Museum purchase with funds donated
by Doris May 2009.2348.1–3

PAGE 38

Man's jacket
Designed by John Pearse (English, born
in 1946) for Granny Takes a Trip
(English, active 1966–1974)
England (London), about 1967
Printed cotton plain weave
74.9 cm (29 1/2 in.)
William Frances Warden Fund 2009.4374

PAGES 40–41

Coquelicot furnishing fabric
Designed by Ken Scott
(American, worked in Italy, 1918–1991)
Italy (Milan), late 1960s
Printed cotton velvet
228.6 x 129.5 cm (90 x 51 in.)
Gift of Giles Kotcher 2003.334

PAGE 41 (RIGHT)

Woman's pantsuit
Designed by Yves Saint Laurent
(French, born in Algeria, 1936–2008) for
Rive Gauche (founded in 1966)
France (Paris), winter 1971
Printed rayon satin
Jacket: 68.6 cm (27 in.); pants: L. 100.3 cm
(39 1/2 in.)
Museum purchase with funds donated
by Doris May 2012.441.1–2

PAGES 42–43

Man's shirt
United States, about 1970
Printed silk plain weave
73.7 cm (29 in.)
Gift of William H. Stover, III 2008.1589

PAGE 49 (LEFT)

Man's suit
Retailed at Granny Takes a Trip
(English, active 1966–1974)
England (London), about 1969–70
Acetate satin weave, cotton velvet, and
cotton twill weave
Jacket: 80 cm (31 1/2 in.); pants: L. 102 cm
(40 in.)
Museum purchase with funds donated
by the Textile and Costume Society,
Museum of Fine Arts, Boston 2010.296.1–2

PAGE 49 (RIGHT)

Man's jacket
Retailed at Granny Takes a Trip
(English, active 1966–1974)
England (London), about 1969–70
Synthetic velvet
78.7 cm (31 in.)
Museum purchase with funds donated
by the Fashion Council, Museum of Fine
Arts, Boston 2007.271

PAGE 51
Dress
Designed by Gina Fratini
(English, born in 1931)
England (London), late 1960s
Printed and embroidered cotton
and polyester gauze, plastic sequins,
and cotton lace
149.9 cm (59 in.)
Anonymous gift 2012.61

PAGE 52
Woman's ensemble
Designed by Adolfo Sardiña, known as
Adolfo (American, born in Cuba, 1933)
United States (New York), about 1970
Printed cotton plain weave
Blouse: 64.1 cm (25¼ in.); skirt: 115.6 cm
(45½ in.)
Museum purchase with funds donated
by Doris May 2010.58.1-2

PAGE 53
Dress
Designed by Betsey Johnson
(American, born in 1942) for Paraphernalia
(American, active 1960s)
United States (New York), 1968
Printed cotton plain weave
141 cm (55½ in.)
Gift of William DeGregorio 2009.2263

PAGES 54-55
Dress
Designed by Thea Porter
(English, born in Jerusalem, 1927-2000)
England (London), about 1970
Printed silk plain weave (chiffon),
rayon and cotton damask, and rayon
velvet ribbon
127 cm (50 in.)
Museum purchase with funds donated by
the Fashion Council, Museum of Fine Arts,
Boston 2007.265

PAGES 57-58
Dress
Designed by Giorgio di Sant'Angelo
(American, born in Italy, 1933-1989)
United States (New York), 1971
Printed synthetic knit (jersey)
152.4 cm (60 in.)
John H. and Ernestine A. Payne Fund
2007.281

PAGE 59
Dress
Designed by Giorgio di Sant'Angelo
(American, born in Italy, 1933-1989)
United States (New York), 1971
Printed polyester plain weave (chiffon)
and polyester knit
149.9 cm (59 in.)
Museum purchase with funds donated by
the Fashion Council, Museum of Fine Arts,
Boston 2007.267

PAGES 60-61
Dress
Designed by Lee Bender (English) for
Bus Stop (English, active 1969-1979)
England (London), about 1970
Printed silk plain weave
144.8 cm (58 in.)
Museum purchase with funds donated by
the Textile and Costume Society, Museum
of Fine Arts, Boston 2008.1041

PAGE 62 (LEFT)
Man's suit
Designed by Norman Stubbs
(American, born in 1943) for East West
Musical Instruments Company
(American, active 1967-1979)
United States (San Francisco), late 1960s
Pieced and appliquéd suede
Jacket: 75 cm (29½ in.); pants: L. 105 cm
(41⁵⁄₁₆ in.)
Museum purchase with funds donated
anonymously and by Stephen Borkowski
in honor of David Lazaro 2009.4976.1-2

PAGE 62 (RIGHT)
Dress
Designed by Zandra Rhodes
(English, born in 1940)
England (London), about 1971
Printed, pierced, and embroidered silk
plain weave
78.7 cm (31 in.)
Museum purchase with funds donated
by Penny Vinik 2008.122

PAGES 64-65
Evening dress
Designed by Bill Blass
(American, 1922-2002)
United States (New York), 1971
Silk plain weave (organza)
130.81 cm (51½ in.)
Museum purchase with funds donated
by the Textile and Costume Society,
Museum of Fine Arts, Boston 2008.343

PAGE 66
Evening gown
Designed by Giorgio di Sant'Angelo
(American, born in Italy, 1933-1989)
United States (New York), early 1970s
Printed silk chiffon with appliquéd
silk flowers
134 cm (53 in.)
Loan Courtesy of the FIDM Museum
at the Fashion Institute of Design
& Merchandising, Los Angeles
Gift of Anonymous Donor

PAGE 67
Dress
Designed by Ossie Clark
(English, 1942-1996)
Fabric designed by Celia Birtwell
(English, born in 1941)
England (London), early 1970s
Printed silk plain weave (crepe)
147.3 cm (58 in.)
Textile Income Purchase Fund 2005.464

PAGE 68
Woman's ensemble
Designed by Bill Gibb (Scottish, 1943-1988)
England (London), autumn-winter 1972
Printed cotton plain weave with rayon pile,
appliquéd snakeskin, and fur
Jacket: 73 cm (28¾ in.); skirt: 85 cm
(33⁷⁄₁₆ in.)
Textile Income Purchase Fund and funds
donated by the Fashion Council, Museum
of Fine Arts, Boston 2009.4375.1-2

PAGES 70-71
Dress
Designed by Bill Gibb (Scottish, 1943-1988)
England (London), 1972
Printed rayon satin
142.2 cm (56 in.)
Gift of Jean S. and Frederic A. Sharf
2011.2324

PAGE 78

Dress
Designed by Ossie Clark
(English, 1942–1996)
Fabric designed by Celia Birtwell
(English, born in 1941)
England (London), 1969–70
Printed acetate and rayon plain weave
(crepe)
124.5 cm (49 in.)
Gift of Mrs. Oric Bates, by exchange
2004.462

PAGE 79

Dress
Designed by Ossie Clark
(English, 1942–1996) for Radley
(English, active 1960–late 1980s)
England (London), about 1970
Acetate and rayon plain weave (crepe)
153 cm (60¼ in.)
Museum purchase with funds by exchange
from the Elizabeth Day McCormick
Collection and donated by the Textile and
Costume Society, Museum of Fine Arts,
Boston 2009.4629

PAGE 80

Lamborghini suit
Designed by Ossie Clark
(English, 1942–1996)
Fabric designed by Celia Birtwell
(English, born in 1941)
England (London), about 1968
Printed cotton and rayon satin
Jacket: 73.7 cm (29 in.);
pants: L. 100.3 cm (39½ in.)
Gift of Jean S. and Frederic A. Sharf
2011.2257.1–2

PAGE 81

Woman's coat
Designed by Ossie Clark
(English, 1942–1996)
England (London), about 1969
Python skin
139.7 cm (55 in.)
Museum purchase with funds donated by
the Fashion Council, Museum of Fine Arts,
Boston 2007.269.1–2

PAGES 84–85

Halter jumpsuit
Designed by Barbara Hulanicki
(English, born in Poland, 1936) for Biba
(English, active 1964–1975)
England (London), early 1970s
Printed diacetate knit
124 cm (49 in.)
Gift of Jean S. and Frederic A. Sharf
2011.2282

PAGE 89

Woman's chubby jacket
Designed by Yves Saint Laurent
(French, born in Algeria, 1936–2008)
for Rive Gauche (founded in 1966)
France (Paris), early 1970s
Marabou feathers and silk plain weave
78.7 cm (31 in.)
Gift of Cherie Acierno in honor of Carol
Weitzner 2010.298

PAGE 90

Dress
Designed by Ossie Clark
(English, 1942–1996)
Fabric designed by Celia Birtwell
(English, born in 1941)
England (London), about 1970
Rayon broken twill (crepe)
102.9 cm (40½ in.)
Museum purchase with funds donated
by the Textile and Costume Society,
Museum of Fine Arts, Boston 2006.1421

PAGE 93

Dress
Designed by Barbara Hulanicki
(English, born in Poland, 1936) for Biba
(English, active 1964–1975)
England (London), early 1970s
Rayon velvet
130.8 cm (51½ in.)
Museum purchase with funds donated by
the Fashion Council, Museum of Fine Arts,
Boston 2012.824

Faux-fur capelet
Designed by Barbara Hulanicki
(English, born in Poland, 1936) for Biba
(English, active 1964–1975)
England (London), early 1970s
Synthetic fur lined with rayon satin
35.6 cm (14 in.)
Gift of Lauren D. Whitley 2012.551

PAGE 98

Man's jacket
Designed by Michael Fish
(English, born in 1940) for Mr. Fish
(English, active 1966–1974)
England (London), about 1970
Wool blend with metallic threads
83.8 cm (33 in.)
The Museum at the Fashion Institute of
Technology, New York
Gift of Wendy Sacks and Joseph Holdner

PAGE 99

Man's caftan
Worn by Rudi Gernreich
(American, born in Austria, 1922–1985)
India, about 1970
Cotton plain weave pieced and
embroidered with cotton threads
and mirrors
135.9 cm (53½ in.)
Loan Courtesy of the FIDM Museum
at the Fashion Institute of Design
& Merchandising, Los Angeles
Bequest of the Rudi Gernreich Estate

PAGE 100

Evening dress
Designed by Arnold Scaasi
(American, born in 1930)
United States (New York), fall 1969
Silk and metallic plain weave with
discontinuous supplementary weft
patterning and continuous supplementary
warp patterning, metal, and silk satin weave
157.5 cm (62 in.)
Arnold Scaasi Collection–Gift of Arnold
Scaasi
Made possible through the generous
support of Jean S. and Frederic A. Sharf,
anonymous donors, Penny and Jeff Vinik,
Lynne and Mark Rickabaugh, Jane and
Robert Burke, Carol Wall, Mrs. I. W.
Colburn, Megan O'Block, Lorraine Bressler,
and Daria Petrilli-Eckert 2009.4032

PAGE 102

Dress
Designed by Thea Porter
(English, born in Jerusalem, 1927–2000)
England (London), about 1969
Tie-dyed and printed silk plain weave
embroidered with metallic and silk yarns
and sequins
151.8 cm (59¾ in.)
Museum purchase with funds donated by
Doris May and Jane Pappalardo 2010.533

Acknowledgments

This book and the exhibition it accompanies could not have been accomplished without the generous assistance and participation of many colleagues and friends. Collectors, curators, registrars, photographers, and of course former hippies across America, the UK, and Europe offered their keen insights and directed me to important sources and collections. I am indebted to Baron Wolman, Geoffrey Aquilina Ross, Iain R. Webb, Judith Watt, Raeanne Rubenstein, Caterine Milinaire, Leslie Verrinder, Carol Troy, Venetia Porter, Caroline Milbank, Colette Harron, Barry Finch, John Robert Miller, Karen Taqi, Stéphane Houy-Towner, Hamish Bowles, Mark and Cleo Butterfield, Martin Price, Romulus von Stezelberger, David Watkins at Goodbye Heart, Joellen Secondo, and Susan Ward for their help. Institutional assistance was efficiently provided by Tom Windross at the Victoria and Albert Museum, Pauline Vidal at the Yves Saint Laurent Foundation, and Chris Royer at the Halston archives. I am especially grateful for the help of Dan Nadel at PictureBox, who provided much-needed contact information for several artists.

I had always heard that early 1970s Tommy Nutter suits were "as rare as hen's teeth," an adage that turned out to be true. However, thanks to lender Peter Brown, the work of the Savile Row innovator is well represented in the exhibition. The participation of several other key lenders has made *Hippie Chic* complete. My gratitude goes to local collector Jimmy Raye, who readily offered to lend pieces from his extraordinary fashion collection, and to Kevin Jones at the Museum of the Fashion Institute of Design and Merchandising in Los Angeles, for his steadfast support for the exhibition, as well as his ebullient assistance all the way through this project. Thanks also to the staff at the Museum of the Fashion Institute of Technology in New York, including Patricia Mears, Fred Dennis, and Sonia Dinghiliam.

Many of the designers who created these extraordinary fashions graciously took time out of their busy schedules to e-mail and speak with me. My thanks go to Barbara Hulanicki, Celia Birtwell, Betsey Johnson, Zandra Rhodes, John Pearse, Stephen Burrows, Ron Atlee, Mirandi Babitz, Charlotte de Vazquez, and Marijke (Kroger) Dunham. One of the pleasures of working on this project was learning more about the East West Musical Instruments Company and the special people who worked at that unique hippie enterprise in San Francisco. Thanks to all the East West folks who generously shared their recollections and enthusiasm, including Norman Stubbs, Carrie Helser, George Golub, Mara Murray, Janis Reed, Larry Fritzlan, and Tim Underwood.

My sincerest gratitude goes to the many donors whose gifts to the MFA form the core of *Hippie Chic*. They include Jean S. and Frederic A. Sharf, Mona Sadler, Bonnie Covington, Jane Pappalardo, Cherie Acierno, Doris May, Elizabeth B. Johnson, Elizabeth Ann Coleman, Stephen Borkowski, Penny Vinik, Giles Kotcher, Lois B. Torf, William DeGregorio, Mr. and Mrs. William C. Van Siclen, Jr., and Cameron Silver. I also must thank The Coby Foundation, Ltd., for its generous support of the exhibition, along with the David and Roberta Logie Fund for Textile and Fashion Arts and the Jean S. and Frederic A. Sharf Exhibition Fund. I am particularly indebted to Ann and John Clarkeson, whose Ann and John Clarkeson Lecture and Publication Fund for Textiles and Costumes provided the means to secure many important images for the catalog. Thanks also to the dedicated members of the Textile and Costume Society and the Fashion Council whose generous funds helped us acquire many signature pieces for the exhibition.

Lastly, I am deeply indebted to my colleagues at the Museum of Fine Arts, Boston, for their expertise and hard work in bringing this project to fruition. Editor Anna Barnet lent her superb editing skills to the publication, maintaining the patience of a saint during the process. Textile Conservators Claudia Iannuccilli and Joel Thompson were enthusiastic about *Hippie Chic* from the beginning and did exceptional work preparing the garments for exhibition and photography. Jill Kennedy-Kernohan ably handled the incoming loans, and Patrick Murphy, Supervisor, Morse Study Room, and Lia and William Poorvu Curatorial Research Fellow, was a great source of psychedelic memorabilia. Brooke Penrose took on the Herculean task of securing image rights and permissions, while Michael Gould met the unique challenges of photographing fashion with skill and equanimity. Special thanks go to Susan Marsh for her brilliant book design, to Tomomi Itakura for her exuberant exhibition layout, and to Emiko Usui, Terry McAweeney, and Jennifer Snodgrass in Publications.

As always, my colleagues in the David and Roberta Logie Department of Textile and Fashion Arts were tremendously helpful and supportive. My sincerest thanks go to Pamela Parmal, Department Head and David and Roberta Logie Curator of Textile and Fashion Arts, Yvonne Markowitz, Rita J. Kaplan and Susan B. Kaplan Curator of Jewelry, Michelle Finamore, Diana Zlatanovski, and Molly Dinnerstein, as well as our dedicated volunteers Gail Smith, Anna Umbreit, Monica Kloppenburg, and Margaret Zoladkowski, who cheerfully provided assistance in scanning images and tracking down information for both the exhibition and this publication. And, finally, to Doris May, our dedicated volunteer, Visiting Committee member, and donor, a heartfelt *merci beaucoup* for all those emails and phone calls to France.

Lauren D. Whitley
Curator, David and Roberta Logie Department of Textile and Fashion Arts

Photography Credits

2–3: Reproduced with permission

6–7: © Fondazione Ken Scott

8–9: Photograph © Raeanne Rubenstein

10: © Henry Diltz / CORBIS

11: Photo by Bill Eppridge / Time & Life Pictures / Getty Images

12: © Everett Collection / Rex USA

13: Photograph © Raeanne Rubenstein

14–15: © Ted Streshinsky / CORBIS

15 (bottom left): Rex USA

15 (bottom right): David Magnus / Rex USA

17: © Chris Morris / Rex / Rex USA

18–19: Photo © Baron Wolman

20 (right): © East West Musical Instruments

25: Courtesy Tessa Traeger

26: © 1967 Neon Rose, www.victormoscoso.com

27 (top): © Keiichi Tanaami

27 (bottom): Reproduced with permission

29: Photography by Brian E. Sanderson. Photograph © FIDM Museum & Library Inc.

30–31: Photography by Brian E. Sanderson. Photograph © FIDM Museum & Library Inc.

32: Pictorial Press Ltd / Alamy

33: BILL ZYGMANT / Rex USA

34–35: Reproduced with permission

38 (left): Photo © Baron Wolman

38 (right): © Bill Zygmant

40–41: © Fondazione Ken Scott

42: © The Museum of Modern Art / Licensed by SCALA / Art Resource, NY

44–45: Courtesy Celia Birtwell

47: Lord Snowdon / *Brides* © The Condé Nast Publications Ltd.

48: Associated Newspapers / Rex USA

49 (top): © Mirror Syndication International

50: Patrick Lichfield / *Vogue*; © Condé Nast

52: Reproduced with permission

53: Charles Bush / *Vogue*; © Condé Nast

54–55: Reproduced with permission

56: Gianni Penati / *Vogue*; © Condé Nast

62 (left): © East West Musical Instruments

62 (right): Reproduced with permission

63: Guy Bourdin / *Vogue* © The Condé Nast Publications Ltd.

66: Photography by Brian E. Sanderson. Photograph © FIDM Museum & Library Inc.

67 (left): Scala / Art Resource, NY

69: *Daily Mail*

74: Photo © Baron Wolman

75: Helmut Newton / *Vogue*; © Condé Nast

76: Courtesy David Nutter

86: Reproduced with permission

87: Jacques Bugat / *Vogue* © The Condé Nast Publications Ltd.

88: © Bruno Barbey / Magnum Photos

94–95: Reproduced with permission

96–97: Terence Donovan Archive / Getty Images

98: © The Museum at FIT

99 (left): Photography by Brian E. Sanderson. Photograph © FIDM Museum & Library Inc.

99 (right): Photo by Hulton Archive / Getty Images

100: © Museum of Fine Arts, Boston

101: Photo by Ron Galella / WireImage

102 (left): Horst / *Vogue*; © Condé Nast

102 (right): Reproduced with permission

103: Reproduced with permission

104: Reproduced with permission

105: Barry Lategan / *Vogue* © The Condé Nast Publications Ltd.

106–7: Reproduced with permission

109: Photo by *Evening Standard* / Getty Images

110 (left): Patrick Lichfield / *Vogue*; © Condé Nast

112: Private collection

116: © The Richard Avedon Foundation

118: Photography by Brian E. Sanderson. Photograph © FIDM Museum & Library Inc. © East West Musical Instruments

119: Charles Tracy / *Vogue*; © Condé Nast

120–21: © East West Musical Instruments

122–23: Horst / *Vogue*; © Condé Nast

124–25: Reproduced with permission

126: Henry Clarke / *Vogue*; © Condé Nast

131: Les Editions Jalou, L'OFFICIEL, 1969

132: © Missoni

133: John Cowan / *Vogue*; © Condé Nast

135–36: Reproduced with permission

137: © East West Musical Instruments

138–39: © East West Musical Instruments. Photograph by Larry Fritzlan

140–141: Reproduced with permission

142: Reproduced with permission

MFA Publications
Museum of Fine Arts, Boston
465 Huntington Avenue
Boston, Massachusetts 02115
www.mfa.org/publications

Published in conjunction with the
exhibition *Hippie Chic*, organized by
the Museum of Fine Arts, Boston,
July 16–November 11, 2013.

The exhibition is supported in part by a
grant from The Coby Foundation, Ltd.

Additional support was provided by the
David and Roberta Logie Fund for Textile
and Fashion Arts and the Jean S. and
Frederic A. Sharf Exhibition Fund.

Generous support for this publication was
provided by the Ann and John Clarkeson
Lecture and Publication Fund for Textile
and Fashion Arts.

While the objects in this publication
necessarily represent only a small portion
of the MFA's holdings, the Museum is
proud to be a leader within the American
museum community in sharing the
objects in its collection via its website.
Currently, information about more than
330,000 objects is available to the public
worldwide. To learn more about the
MFA's collections, including provenance,
publication, and exhibition history,
kindly visit *www.mfa.org/collections.*

For a complete listing of MFA
publications, please contact the publisher
at the above address, or call 617 369 3438.

Front cover: Fashions and interior by
The Fool at the Beatles' Apple Boutique
(1967). Photograph by Ronald Traeger.
Courtesy Tessa Traeger.

Back cover (left to right): Details from
pages 58, 67, 54, 34, 106, and 71.

*The use of images of individuals, famous
and otherwise, throughout this publication
is for editorial and informational purposes
only. Such use should in no way be
understood to imply any sort of affiliation
with, sponsorship by, or endorsement by
any person or person(s) featured in this
publication.*

All garments from the collections of the
Museum of Fine Arts, Boston, in this book
were photographed by the Museum's
Imaging Studios.

Edited by Anna Barnet
Copyedited by Amanda Heller
Proofread by Dalia Geffen
Designed by Susan Marsh
Typeset by Matt Mayerchak in Archer
Production by Terry McAweeney
and Anna Barnet
Printed and bound at Graphicom,
Verona, Italy

Available through ARTBOOK | D.A.P.
155 Sixth Avenue, 2nd floor
New York, New York 10013
Tel.: 212 627 1999 | Fax: 212 627 9484
www.artbook.com

First edition
Printed and bound in Italy
This book was printed on acid-free paper.

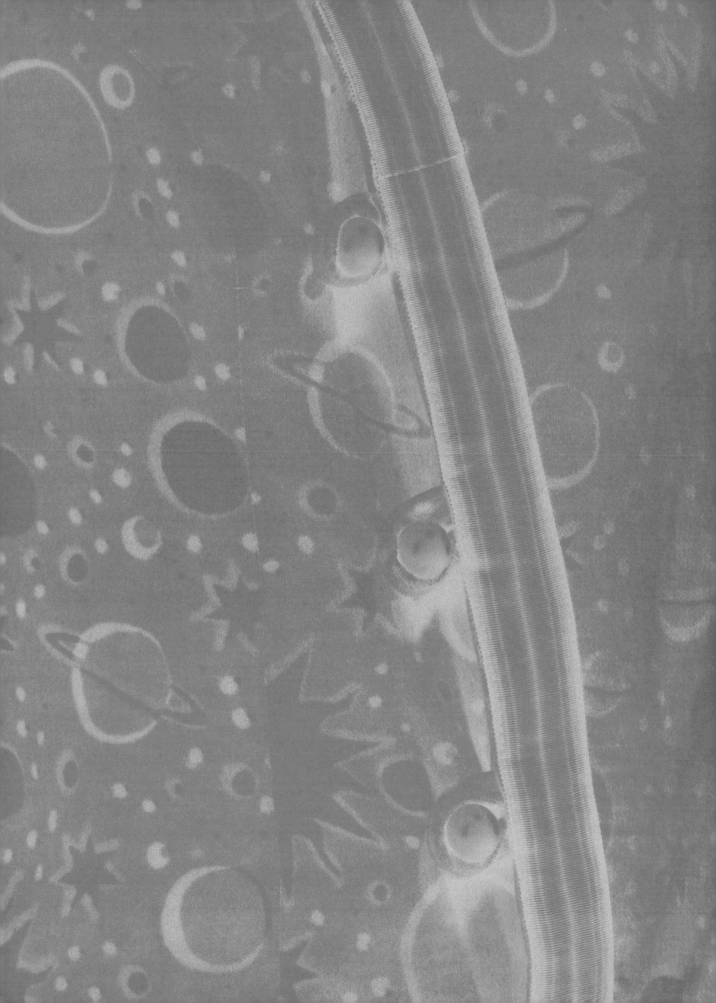

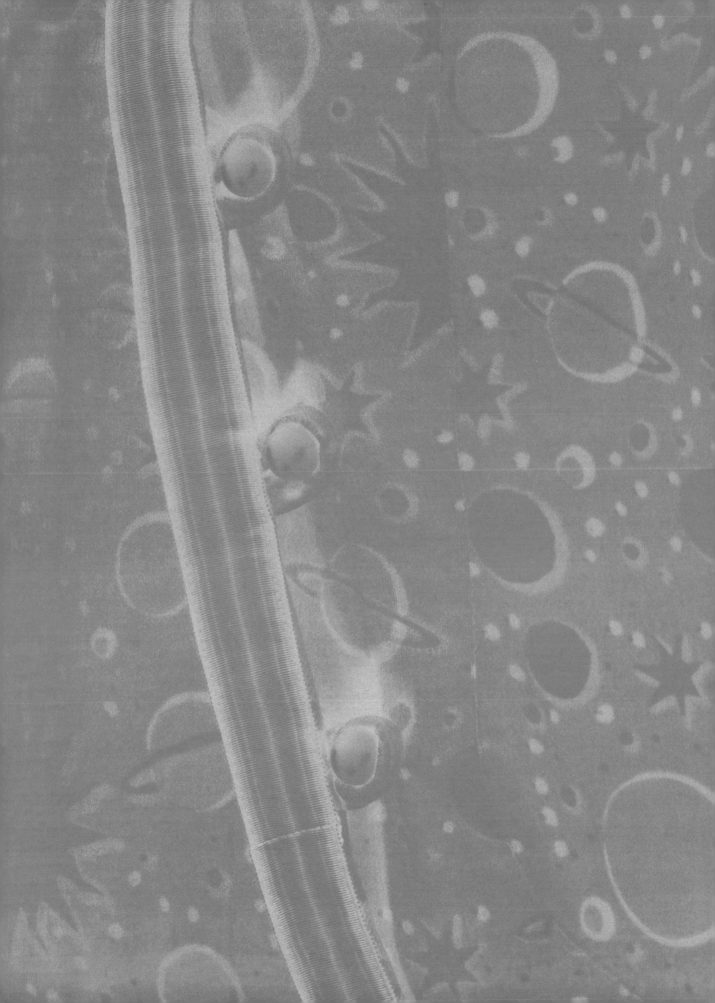